The Aftermath of Hurricane Katrina

Educating Traumatized Children Pre-K through College

Edited by
Dorothy M. Singleton

D1571987

UNIVERSITY PRESS OF AMERICA,® INC.
Lanham • Boulder • New York • Toronto • Plymouth, UK

Copyright © 2008 by
University Press of America,® Inc.
4501 Forbes Boulevard
Suite 200
Lanham, Maryland 20706
UPA Acquisitions Department (301) 459-3366

Estover Road
Plymouth PL6 7PY
United Kingdom

Library of Congress Control Number: 2007943311
ISBN-13: 978-0-7618-3999-6 (paperback : alk. paper)
ISBN-10: 0-7618-3999-2 (paperback : alk. paper)

Contents

Preface

The Hurricane Katrina floods were a series of tragic events that left a trail of destruction that will be there for sometime. The lack of government response, at the local, state, and the national level was indeed unexpected and tragic. People all over the world were forced to see the poverty that existed all of the time, but was covered up as people concentrated upon the joyful sections of town. Many New Orleans natives are all over the nation, some with no hopes of returning home. The French Quarter sections have been renovated and Mardi Gras has continued on as before. There was not a time or money to entirely replace the flood walls with higher and stronger ones. We are now hearing reports from the National Corps of Engineers and the National Science Foundation teams that the French Quarter is at greater risk than before Katrina. Damaged Creole cottages in Treme, a lovely neighborhood that is next to the French Quarter, where plantation owners once housed their Black mistresses, now looks as if Treme and the French Quarter are at risk for flooding. The tragedy of Katrina will continue with even greater losses in the future.

Harriette Pipes McAdoo

Introduction: Educating Traumatized Children and Adolescents

Dorothy M. Singleton

There has been so much hype with Hurricane Katrina during the year 2005. Two years later, the people in the gulf coast area are still experiencing trauma and despair which have turned their lives upside down. Where was the aid when they needed it? We can talk about history as it was a long time ago, and we can talk about history as it is today. Has anything changed? Does America really care about its people?

The National Institute of Mental Health (2001) defines "trauma" as both a medical and a psychiatric definition. Medically, "trauma" refers to a serious or critical bodily injury, wound, or shock. This definition is often associated with trauma medicine practiced in emergency rooms and represents a popular view of the term. Psychiatrically, "trauma" has assumed a different meaning and refers to an experience that is emotionally painful, distressful, or shocking, which often results in lasting mental and physical effects. Can you image the trauma the people of the gulf coast region have experienced?

When I arrived in New Orleans, Louisiana on May 6, 2006, the faces of people varied (happy, tensed, frowns, sad, and signs of being disgusted). There were people sitting on porches; riding bicycles along the untidy streets; and there were people driving different model cars like anyone else in a city. The environment was unlike anything I've ever seen in my life. People were moving about as though they were among the "walking dead." New Orleans, Louisiana looked as though it was part of a third world country; not like America, the land of plenty.

The purpose of this book is to examine the impact of how Hurricane Katrina has traumatized children and what effects it has on their academic progression, socialization opportunities, and social consciousness; and to better understand teaching strategies and methodologies of working with traumatized children in Pre-kindergarten through college classrooms.

As writers gathered information for this book, several of them stated that given the events of the past two years and the catastrophic impact of Hurricane Katrina upon the Gulf Coast and the families that call this area home, there is a need to better understand how this environmental tragedy has disrupted the lives of groups already politically and economically marginalized. The chapter on *Things Fall Apart: African American Families in New Orleans Responding to Hurricane Katrina* will discuss the unique history, culture, and family life of African Americans in New Orleans as well as the challenges these families face as their entire community is currently in influx. Social scientists and human service professionals can help rebuild the lives of these families in the Gulf Coast region.

Other writers of this book reported that "American society, since its inception, has been based upon the fundamental principles that all citizens are entitled to life, liberty and the pursuit of happiness (Declaration of Independence)." These fundamental principles are steeped in the notion of liberalism and the First Amendment of the U.S. Constitution—the rights of individuals to freely express their opinions as well as the right of individuals to assemble to express ones "views." Within this context, the basic tenets of social capital emerged as individuals began to exercise their unalienable rights.

Hurricane Katrina made a bad situation even worst. According to the U.S. Department of Education, the hurricane displaced 372,000 students and approximately 700 schools have been damaged or destroyed. Over 50 percent of schools have reopened in New Orleans, meeting population needs. Students and personnel data, school district information systems, instructional materials and equipment, and other valuable resources need to be recovered or replaced with government's assistance.

On January 18, 2006, US Secretary of Education Margaret Spellings visited New Orleans. She met with leaders of eight major New Orleans institutions of higher education affected by the hurricanes (Rita and Katrina). They were Scott Cowen, president, Tulane University; Marvelene Hughes, president, Dillard University; Norman Francis, president, Xavier University; the Rev. Kevin Wildes, president, Loyola University; Tommy Warner, chancellor, Nunez Community College; Alex Johnson, chancellor, Delgado Community College; Victor Ukpolo, chancellor, Southern University; and, Tim Ryan, chancellor, University of New Orleans. Students from each college also attended the meeting, sharing the challenges they faced last semester and their thoughts as they start the spring semester at their home. The Bush Administration and Secretary Spellings have initiated numerous efforts to benefit students and colleges affected by the hurricanes, including assistance in repaying student loans and flexibility in awarding financial aid (US Department of Education, 2006). All major institutions of higher education in the region have reopened (US Department of Education, April 2007). In short, this book will capture the devastating effects of Hurricane Katrina on education and the welfare of children and youth; and as well as families and community members at large. This book, also, will emphasize lessons learned from the devastating effects of Hurricane Katrina and how educators can help children and youth progress, psychologically, academically, and socially.

Trauma—Age-defined Groups: The National Institute of Mental Health (2001) has identified the following groups of children and adolescents and several characteristics of trauma.

For children 5 years of age and younger, typical reactions can include a fear of being separated from the parent, crying, whimpering, screaming, immobility and/or aimless motion, trembling, frightened facial expressions and excessive clinging. Parents may also notice children returning to behaviors exhibited at earlier ages (these are called regressive behaviors), such as thumb-sucking, bedwetting, and fear of darkness. Children in this age bracket tend to be strongly affected by the parents' reactions to the traumatic event.

Children 6 to 11 years old may show extreme withdrawal, disruptive behavior, and/or inability to pay attention. Regressive behaviors, nightmares, sleep problems, irrational fears, irritability, refusal to attend school, outbursts of anger and fighting are also common in traumatized children of this age. Also the child may complain of stomachaches or other bodily symptoms that have no medical basis. Schoolwork often suffers. Depression, anxiety, feelings of guilt and emotional numbing or "flatness" is often present as well.

Adolescents 12 to 17 years old may exhibit responses similar to those of adults, including flashbacks, nightmares, emotional numbing, avoidance of any reminders of the traumatic event, depression, substance abuse, problems with peers, and anti-social behavior. Also common are withdrawal and isolation, physical complaints, suicidal thoughts, school avoidance, academic decline, sleep disturbances, and confusion. The adolescent may feel extreme guilt over his or her failure to prevent injury or loss of life, and may harbor revenge fantasies that interfere with recovery from the trauma.

The National Institute of Mental Health (2001) continues to explain that after violence or a disaster occurs, the family is the first-line resource for helping. Among the things that parents and other caring adult can do are:

- Explain the episode of violence or disasters as well as you are able.
- Encourage the children to express their feelings and listen without passing judgment. Help younger children learn to use words that express their feelings. However, do not force discussion of the traumatic event.
- Let children and adolescents know that it is normal to feel upset after something bad happens.

- Allow time for the youngsters to experience and talk about their feelings. At home, however, a gradual return to routine can be reassuring to the child.
- If your children are fearful, reassure them that you love them and will take care of them. Stay together as a family as much as possible.
- If behavior at bedtime is a problem, give the child extra time and reassurance. Let him or her sleep with a light on or in your room for a limited time if necessary.
- Do not criticize regressive behavior or shame the child with words like "babyish."
- Allow children to cry or be sad. Don't expect them to be brave or tough.
- Encourage children and adolescents to feel in control. Let them make some decisions about meals, what to wear, etc.
- Take care of yourself so you can take care of the children.

Some of the pointers to remember about educating traumatized children and adolescents are 1) consider all problematic behavior within the context of coping to better understand "why the child (ren) keeps doing that"?, 2) repetition is important because with every positive experience there is a positive response (intrinsic/extrinsic reward), allow the child (ren) explore their feelings through kinesthetic activities, and 3) DON'T GIVE UP HOPE!

At one time in our life, we have experience some type of trauma. How we manage to deal with it was totally left up to us. We had to develop coping and problem-solving skills for managing anxiety. It is necessary to get help from counselors, psychologists and human services professionals. Remember the pointers stated in this chapter.

BIBLIOGRAPHY

National Institute of Mental Health (2001); http://www.nimh.nih.gov/publicat/violence
    .cfm
U.S. Department of Education (2006, 2007); www.ed.gov

Chapter One

Conceptual Framework for Developing Cultural Identity among African Americans

Phillip Masila Mutisya and Carl Robinson

ABSTRACT

It needs no emphasis that "Africans have been so buffeted, displaced, manipulated and degraded" through the years of "slave trade, imperial conquest, resource despoliation, and economic marginalization that the African has reached a depth of despair and wretchedness." This pathetic situation often "translates into POVERTY: poverty of direction, poverty of imagination, and poverty of power of enterprising vision. This being the case, if we as Africans are to move forward, "we must recreate our own self-designed road to material richness and psychic or cultural peace." We have no choice but to find our lost glory. We hold the key to our success and prosperity. But when we redefine where we come from shall we know where we are going (Ogutu, 2000).

This chapter will include a discussion on conceptual aspects that we propose as a guideline for re-conceptualization of African American cultural identity as a means to cultural emancipation from Eurocentric marginalization. A conceptual framework is direly needed that would serve as a renaissance that places people of African descent at a common memory or NTU, the essence of being as a people that Ogutu (2000) echoes to the quote above. There have been many efforts put forth to revitalize Africans and African Americans' cultural identity, however, such effort center on reactive or pathological symptoms and not on causes and effects. Thus, a focus on a more proactive perspective would lead to a real renaissance which the Afrocentric theory has already started to address in this century.

The conceptual aspects discussed in this chapter will include philosophical beliefs and practical strategies that can be applied to truly engage a dialectal

1

process that is truly needed for reconstruction of African American cultural identity from European marginalization to an Afrocentric centered perspective or NTU. Specific aspects will include an examination of thought and practice as a means of reconceptualization of African culture and identity from a pathological perspective to a more positive world view; and an examination of the contradictions that impact African Americans negatively as far as education, economics, and social, political and psychological perspectives. The discussion in the chapter will also include suggestions on strategies that are aimed at empowering people in combating these contradictions through conscientizacao process that helps people learn how to perceive the contradictions in their lives and begin to transform society creatively.

INTRODUCTION

This chapter is written in response to the Aftermath of Katrina which led to the need of developing a collaborative effort among colleagues to create a book that will not only be geared to responding to Katrina disaster, but also to serve as a healing process. This chapter thus, includes a discussion of conceptual aspects that we believe set a beginning on developing such a process, that we believe is a basis of recovery from traumas of Katrina and the pre-existing internalized oppression by people of African decent. It is a our strong belief that poverty or crises no matter how severe they are do not retard or handicap individuals' ability to survive, and neither does it destroy ones identity especially if an individual or individuals in the society have an identity, but internalized oppression does affect ones identity or individuals in a society if not interrupted. For example, the majority of the world is poor and that has not affected most people in terms of identity or who they are as people not matter what crises they have faced. Thus, the Katrina crises did not create a crisis in identity among people of African decent but did start a dialogue that reveals the need to identify ways in which we can collectively respond to the way African Americans are treated in this country. It also augmented the need to combat the internalized oppression more seriously.

The Katrina aftermath also revealed the vacuum that exists in and among the African Americans and how they are treated in the American society. It has heightened the awareness regarding the dire need for reframing and conceptualization of a positive ways in which the African Americans or people of African decent need to wake up and think, individually and collectively in educating their own people about the oppressive conditions that they live in regardless of all levels of status: social, economic, educational or political. The urgency in thinking is critical and because of the depth and longevity the internalization has taken place would need more than rhetoric but a serious dialogue based on tried and tested methods.

Critical pedagogy approach approached from Afrocentric perspective is a viable means to bring solutions to this the identity crisis that people of African decent face in all fronts; in education, economic, social, political and especially the impact the crisis has on the people psychologically after internalizing it for a long time. Thus, re-educating the masses about this serious persistent problem has to be approached from all fronts involving all the parties who have a stake in it including: the parents, teachers, and policy makers in education and economic planning of the society.

If we compare Katrina crisis to the crises that occur in other countries we can see that the crises never affects the identity of the people in most societies, especially where people have not been as dehumanized as has been the case in the United States of America; and mostly countries where hegemony has been the mainstay. The issue with Katrina is that the identity crisis existed before the event caused by the hurricane. Mutisya and Mbuva (2006) in an introductory chapter of the book "Conceptualizing African and African American Family and Identity Development: Intra-cultural, Inter-cultural and Cross-cultural Perspectives" have laid a foundation on developing a constructive conceptualization of identity development by addressing the main source of the problem that impedes a positive approach by pointing out that:

Most literature or books on studies on black family (African Americans and Africans) are theory based and provide limited view or realistic aspects that shape African and African American family as a concept from a positive approach. The limitations are due to the fact that the approaches in writing or conducting research have been reactive in nature and do not provide a conceptual framework that is positive and realistic in describing either African, or African American, because most approaches are Eurocentric in perspective, and hegemonic driven that negates the possibility of viewing people of African decent from their world view, and positively. Such view, we believe treats African people in comparison to European contexts or from a pathological perspective that has led to marginalization of African peoples' identity in the continent and its Diaspora to Europeans (Asante, 1993, Wathiong'o, 1986, Khalid, 1977).

They further point out that:

Therefore, an African and African American positive context misperceptions are created from the misinterpretation, or due to linguistic differences, language and miscommunication in conducting research and the inappropriate approaches. To some extend, some distortions of both African and African American culture have been intentional due to hegemony driven approach either through slavery in America or colonialism in Africa. Thus, the focus on research on the relationship between Africans and African Americans as far as cultural identity is concerned has not received much attention because in the last 40 years the research interest and development have been shaped by the reactionary approach due to colonialism and its negative impact and how to reform the education system. The reactive nature has also been shaped by blaming the west or the former colonialists/ Europeans and or as in the case with African Americans, former slave owners.

Ngugi Wathiong'o (1986) points out that values are the basis of a peoples' identity, their sense of particularity as members of the human race which is carried by language. He also asserts that language as culture is the collective memory bank of a peoples experience in history, and culture is almost indistinguishable from the language that makes possible its genesis, growth, banking, articulation and indeed its transmission from one generation to the next. Further, he indicates that culture transmits or imparts those images of the world and reality through the spoken and written language, that is, through a specific language. Thus, language is viewed as both communication and culture, and a product of each other. Notably, in the process of making in America Language and culture were the main aspects taken away and were replaced by an internalized oppression that has been passed down to several generation due to the systemic racism in the society. Thus, to approach reconstruction of identity of African American from pathological perspective to a more positive view requires more than status quo.

Almost all Africans were colonized at one time or another by Europeans. Colonization impacted most Africans in many ways, especially the youth. A serious assort occurred to suppress traditional values indigenous to the people, and substituted those values with new values, or westernization (Europeanization). It is sometimes difficult to measure identity development in adolescents and young adults, especially those reared under the remnants of colonialism (or slavery as in America) because the methods that were appropriate to measure the identity development are not congruent to the culture. One fact is that under the remnants of colonialism in Africa, some individuals group of people have kept their traditional values, whereas others have become more or less acculturated with the former colonist traditions and values, specifically, the importance of preserving one's or group identity. To some extend, some African Americans have retained some of these values but are faced with continuous alienation due to the mainstream hegemony driven culture that tents to suppress any effort aimed at revitalization of the positive aspects of identity development.

Thus it is important to know which variables predict those values and the differences in order to pass down to the next generation. However, for African

Americans marginalization has continued due to hegemony that has prevailed in the society resulting to internalization of oppressive conditions that have been passed down to both the oppressor and oppressed; due to lack of a constructive and culturally responsive revitalization of identity development with values that empower or humanize people of African decent. Colonialism or slavery was not intended to empower its subjects but to marginalize them through "divide and conquer" methods as described in Willy Lynch in the West, Fraser (1994). Post colonialism gave mere rhetoric to the reform movement, which resulted in economic, educational, social and cultural dependency marginal to Europeans. This was done through coercion during the colonial era, and now voluntarily by post neocolonialists in Africa. In America, post-slavery has taken the similar directions despite many efforts to revitalize the humanity that has been marginalized through hegemony. An example is the revolution that took place in the sixties now appears to be so remote that one wonders whether it was just a myth or a reality. There are many reasons why the movement did not continue. However, we believe one of the main reason is that the framework used by the people was not transformative in approach and had not sustainable core values that shaped ideology that would prevail against in spite of the assort to the movement by racism in the society. Most of the strategies worked but were based on rhetoric and lacked sustainable ideology, and were based on blame. Thus, once the continuity warranted constructive approach that would maintain it, it failed. However, some positive development emerged that led to the birth of Afrocentricity as a viable concept and theory.

THEORETICAL AND PHILOSOPHICAL PERSPECTIVES

Hernandez-Sheets and Hollins (1999) assert that human development in the United States of America mainly uses four theories: the Psychoanalytic by Erickson 1950, and Freud 1940, Behavioral by Skinner 1957, humanistic by Maslow1968, Rogers 1970, and cognitive by Bandura1977, Piaget 1952. These theories are not only relatively new and monocultural but also rooted in U.S individualism. As far as ethnicity is concerned, ethnic groups, and ethnic identity differ considerably when studied from different theoretical and disciplinary perspective that is phenomenology, sociology, anthropology, archaeology, education and psychology (Hernandez-Sheets and Hollins (1999) p. 91). Not only are these theories limited but they are Eurocentric in perspective, however, they are treated as universal in the American society. They further point that the conceptualization of these constructs is also influenced by other factors. They include the particular aspects being researched, the area in the world where the research takes place, the particular group under investigation, the value orientation of the researcher, and the perceived sociological and cultural position of the group under study.

The above theories fail to address and tend to marginalize both Africans as well as African Americans, which suggests a creation or reconstruction of a different and positive way to conceptualize identity of people of African decent in America. Mutisya and Ross (2006) attempted to empirically operationalized Afrocentricity as a concept to a theory; and by supporting (Asante, 1988) suggests Afrocentricity as one of the positive ways to conceptualize a framework that includes Africans as subjects rather than objects of inquiry. The Afrocentric perspective incorporates Africans at the center of the study rather than on the periphery. Afrocentricity as a methodological tool includes appropriate definition of the identity concepts such as ethnicity and race. The following definition of ethnic identity adapted by Hernandez-Sheets and Hollins is more appropriate to Africans and those of the African Diaspora.

A collective with in a larger society having real or putative common ancestry, memories of a shared historical past, and cultural focus on one of more symbolic elements defined as the epitome of their people hood. Examples of such symbolic elements are: kingship patterns, physical contiguity as in localism or sectionalism, religious affiliation, language or dialect forms, tribal affiliation, nationality, phenotypic features, or any combination of these. A necessary accompaniment is some consciousness of kind among members of the group (Hernandez-Sheets and Hollins, 1999).

This perspective of identity is necessary however; it is ignored by (magical) explanations that are given when it comes to reconstructing or reclaiming African American identity that is aimed at empowering them to be centered in a positive worldview, as opposed to the one marginal to European. Thus, the "status quo" remains for lack of a constructive and culturally responsive identity development framework that empowers and humanizes instead of de-humanization of people of African decent in America. Due to the lack of such a framework, identity formation for African Americans therefore is conceptualized from physical characteristics that are de-humanizing because they are based on either or superficial aspects that are stereotypical and materialistic in nature. Therefore, socialization of youth leads to pathological worldview that leads one to identity that is characterized by physical attributes and material possession (Bling Bling), which are measures of oppression and marginalization of a people in a society. Thus, it is not surprising to see what prevails today whereby one is socialized to ignore the important aspects of identity, such as a name, culture and moral values. For example, when you ask one "who are you," you are likely to hear what that person does as a response. This view thus, results from internalization of one's identity in material sense, then it is no wonder that most African American or any oppressed people are viewed or view themselves as poor or rich in material terms when referring to their identity.

Jedlicka (2005) attempted to address the dilemma in defining and developing theories of identity from ethnic and racial by reviewing the existing theories and the challenges in conceptualizing ones or group identity. However, he cautions the use the word "race," by asserting that "The word "race" is one of the most meaningless and useless words ever uttered in the English language. To never use the word again, or to never hear anyone else use it again, is to lose nothing of value." However, as Jedlicka (2005) points out, the conflicts that arise when conceptualizing identity from racial and ethnic perspective, by asserting that, using race as a construct in developing a theoretical framework is not only flawed but confusing because of using a socially constructed concept that is used synonymously with ethnicity. Jedlicka (2005) used an example of J.E. Helms who defines racial identity as a person's ability to identify with the racial group with which he or she is generally assumed to share racial heritage. Mutisya and Ros (2006) study found that Afrocentricity and racial social socialization has an impact rather than racial socialization a lone, however, race is still used as a construct to define identity in many cases which is flawed and confusing. Mutisya and Ross (2006) study confirmed Jedlicka (2005) assertion that:

> As children learn to think, by age seven or eight, they may develop "reflexive intelligence." Reflexivity refers to the process by which a person comes to know one self through introspection and through interactions with others. Reflexive ethnic identity develops when the person sees one's own ethnic image in the way others see him or her. Taking on parents' ethnic attitudes, and the sharing of those attitudes develops an ethnic identity in children. This awareness of seeing oneself as others do occurs when the attitudes of the parents become one's own. Rosenberg (1990) argues that Mead (1934) and Cooley (1902) "showed clearly that reflexivity among human beings is rooted in the social process, particularly the process of taking the role of the other and of seeing the self from the other's perspective" (p. 3). (Davor, 200 . . . P. 6)

Jedlicka (2005) further stresses that "*The* process of identity development is responsible for the transference of ethnic identity from one generation to the next. When parents do not fulfill that role, ethnic attitudes about self and others tend to be learned from peers, the media, and schools. Even when the parents are socializing their children, other socializing agents can either support or counter parental influences." (P. 6) Jedlicka (2005) also points out that beliefs about one's own physical traits or race can be the basis for the formation of ethnic groups. "Race" as an element of ethnic identity without an associated belief, is no more than a socially constructed, ethnic category. One's awareness of being categorized, however, is enough for a person to have a sense of ethnic identity based on race. Beliefs about the virtues, history or migration of a race, according to Weber, facilitate ethnic (P. 5).

Identity development is something that all African American youths will have to face, but they will go through the stages at different times in their lives and at different rates. Marshall (2002) drawing from Banks theory describes stages of identity development that we believe are essential in developing a conceptual framework. Marshall (2002) asserts that forming a healthy personal identity is important for all ethnic minority youths to ensure academic success, but also for them to have positive feelings about themselves so they can enjoy all aspects of life. She further describes three stages of identity development ethnic minority youths will go through: 1) unexamined ethnic identity, 2) ethnic identity search, and 3) ethnic identity achievement. During the first stage, adolescents have not self reflected and do not think about the importance that ethnicity plays in their lives and they do not have an interest in learning more about their ethnicity. During the second stage, adolescents are beginning to explore more about ethnicity and the role in plays in their lives and the lives of other in society. In this second stage they begin to become aware of some of the difficulties that minorities face in our society. During the final stage of identity development, adolescents have done self reflection and have explored their own ethnicity and how it impacts their lives and others. They have faced the negative stereotypes and difficulties that are associated with their ethnicity and have come to terms with them.

Traditional teacher training education has no set strategies or curriculum that teachers can follow to be successful when working with African Americans, but there are some common characteristics that successful teachers have in common. Successful teachers have high self efficacy and believe that what they do will impact the success their student will or will not have in the classroom. These teachers believe that all students are capable of being successful and have high expectations for all their students. Successful teachers pay attention to the personal lives of their students and respect their students' feelings, attitudes, and previous experiences. They do not just teach the textbook curriculum, they teach "the whole child." Successful teachers use a variety of teaching styles to meet the diverse needs of their students and include opportunities for students to be actively involved in constructing knowledge and participating in cooperative learning groups. Successful teachers use the arts as a way to liven up the classroom and engage students by tapping on their cultural styles.

When teachers include music, dance, drama, and other aspects of different cultures into their teaching, students feel a connection with the curriculum and are more motivated to learn. Successful teachers respect themselves, their students, and their profession by always making sure their outside appearance reflects the pride they feel inside (Thus centered in their world view) as well. Successful teachers make connections with their students by learning about the students' backgrounds and finding areas in the curriculum that connect to their lives and prior experiences. They also make connections with their students by forming relationships in their communities outside of school so they can learn more about their students' background from the adults in the black communities (Marshall, (2002), and Banks, (2000).

It therefore important for African American parents and educators to develop healthy racial identities about themselves because it impacts their interpersonal actions the school communities in which they work. When parents and educators are able to form healthy racial identities, they are able to understand and appreciate who they are and place themselves in a position to better understand and appreciate the differences that exist in other people that surround them in their school communities. To have genuine relationships with people in their school community who may have different cultural backgrounds, they must understand their own cultural background before they attempt to understand and appreciate some one else's cultural background. Understanding their cultural perspective in this respect it means being centered in a world view that humanizes and empowers them. Mutisya and Ross (2006) findings on Afrocentricity and racial socialization supports the approach that incorporates racial socialization centered in a worldview.

Nichols Model (Philosophical Cultural Differences)

Beck (2002) in "The Creative Proportion between the World Cultures" article published in the "Thought and Practice in African Philosophy" points us to the centrality of philosophy role on conceptualizing education.

Not least because of the rapid development of modern technology, the traditional cultures have entered worldwide into communication and interaction. The mutual affection and dependence is growing in diverse areas: not only in economics and politics, but also in sciences and arts, as well as in philosophy and religion.

He goes farther to assert that the evolution of mankind seems to tend to create "global unity" of mutual exchange between continents and cultures on all levels of life, in which the ethnological differences and each individual identity of people should not be leveled out or even be eliminated, but conserved and integrated, albeit in a an altered form (P. 63). He suggests that, this aim can be presented by the idea of dynamic and creative world peace, where by, the order is not imposed violently from outside or above, but which is far more founded from the inside, in as far as it corresponds to the basic disposition of human beings, and therefore advances mankind in being human and in being humane. In this respect, Beck is right when he warns that "In any other way, the survival of mankind seems to be impossible, as the destruction potential of technology is growing inexorably and the 'lebensraum (space of life) is getting scarce." He farther stresses that; such peace would imply a living in unity of mutual appreciation and completion in the diversity and variety of ways of life. He also indicates, this peace cannot manifest itself in the long run as a monotone standardized culture as in the Western Societies, which is a forced form of an intellectual and ideological 'absolutes monism' which would suppress or obstruct free individual development of people (P. 63).

Beck (2002) and others have identified the serious need for examining the theories that have influenced education systems in both USA and the rest of the world, in this case, Kenya and Africa, and from a global perspectives in order to arrive to viable reform process that is sustainable, and addresses the perceived contradictions that the education systems face. Ogutu (2002) in his article "African Renaissance: A Third Millennium Challenge to Thought and Practice in African Philosophy" points out the dilemmas African institutions face in their conceptualization of educational development:

"Following political independence, the emergent African states established universities modeled on those of the west. The pioneer 'Masters' were trained in Britain, France, and Portugal. Some of them have remained more European than the Europeans themselves"

Ogutu's caution points out a very important question that African institutions are facing today, which also poses a similar question for African Americans' health and identity development, who are equally faced with the challenge of what beliefs, or theoretical/Philosophical approach that is/are appropriate to use in reforming their educational system or that is culturally responsive (Billingsley, 1981). The same case applies to Africa in terms of what changes need to be addressed, and what theoretical frameworks are appropriate to use to draw an Intra-cultural, cross-cultural, and intercultural awareness/consciousness for both Africans and African Americans and the African Diaspora as whole? Observation leads us to believe that there is a dire need for establishing a viable and sustainable framework that is focused on humanizing educational development that would lead to a viable and sustainable economic, socio-cultural, political and psychological wellbeing for Africans and its Diaspora, and that leads to identity development that is not "marginal to European."

Freire (1994) developed such methods in "Pedagogy of the Oppressed" and in many other works based on his method of concientizacao that helps participants in learning to perceive contradictions that arise as a result of the miss-education in terms of education: Economic, social and psychological perspectives. Smith, (1978) also made a contribution by operationalizing Freire's methods (Concientizacao) in his dissertation whereby he came up with simple and useful instrument that can be used to determine the levels of consciousness in engaging people in the process of humanizing education process (Concientizacao, or critical conscious approach to dialogue). Critical pedagogy has emerged as a result that may bring a health discussion and as means of developing culturally responsive and sustainable cultural identity development, especially for those who have been marginalized through hegemony. The following sets of questions adapted from (Smith, 1978) form concientizacao process:

Paulo Freire, through his work in the slums of Brazil, began to conceptualize a process of conscious-raising leading toward a dynamic concept of liberation and towards what he refers to as a more complete humanness. The product of this process he calls Conscientizacao. A degree of consciousness in which individuals are able to see the social system critically. They are able to understand the resultant contradictions in their own lives, and to generalize those contradictions to others around them and transform society creatively with others. The process is coded into three levels: Magical, Naïve and Critical: Magical-Naïve-Critical. The process question include three parts: Naming, Reflecting and Acting.

Naming involves responding to these sets of questions:

What are the most pressing problems in your life or in your teaching profession right now?
Should things be as they are?
How should they be?
(Relate these questions to the problems you find in your profession that are dehumanizing or impact your work or what you do negatively).

Reflecting involves responding to these sets of questions:

Why are things this way?
Who is to blame?
What is your role in the situation?
Acting involves responding to these sets of questions
What can be done?
What should be done?
What have you done or will you do?

After all the participants in the dialogue group writes down responses to these questions, the next step involves dialectical discussion in a safe place where every ones opinion is respected. The process however, has to be facilitated by trained individuals.

DIFFERENCES BETWEEN EUROCENTRIC APPROACH AND AFRICAN IN THOUGHT PROCESS

As part of conceptualization of this discussion we must consider the philosophical cultural differences between European and African identity development. Richard (1993) points out the important aspect on developing a conceptual framework:

> *Successful intercultural communication and interaction does not usually occur by chance. Rather, it is the result of exchanges and behavior on the part of the persons who not only desire favorable results but have the skills necessary for generating and supporting positive outcomes. These skills may be yours-now or later-but, for success, a planned framework for their development is essential Conceptual Framework is a "Consciously organized arrangements of related information that, because we are aware of them, influence our actions.*

He further states that, the degree to which we understand our own frameworks and the frameworks of others is often the degree to which we achieve unthreatened and successful human interactions. Thus, our own personal frameworks are often determined by our cultures and to understand the significance of this observation, we must have an understanding of culture in general because we all view our world thorough culturally influenced frameworks that often collide with the different frameworks of others, which creates a conflict and thus we feel threatened. Beck, (2002) describes the opposition between the European, African, and Asian cultures that help in explaining the impact of thought and practice that have resulted to conflicts with the nature and existence for Africans and African Americans. This explains some of the causes for the disparities in attitudes and perception of Africans and African Americans towards affirming and reconstruction of identity development and a means to dealing with oppressive conditions in the American society.

> *Being the expression and actualization of human spiritual life, every culture depends on physical-material conditions, that is, basically, on the structure of the surface of the earth and on the climate. In this sense, culture, so to speak, means the human mind's response to the demanding and provoking challenges given by nature.*

He points that, "apparently, this dialogue between mind and nature partially succeeds; partially, however, it fails. For it is actualized always by interplay of two components:

> *On the one hand, the full "ac-tuality" of nature consists in its effects carried out on humanity, and humans have to receive this acting actuality and take it in. This actuality is "addressing" each person, and the person, and the person has to "listen." But then, on the other hand, one can act back on it and give the "Re-sponse," by articulating oneself in the direction of nature and into nature, forming and determining it, thus actualizing and objectivating ones ideas and ones will. Thus concrete culture appears to be an always more or less fitting and adequate reaction of humanity towards what nature gives us (P. 65).*

Beck adds that, this might signify that the world as a meaningful whole, and as an "onto-logical" structure comprehending nature and culture, and how the structure is actualized more or less in accordance with its meaning, depends on the historical dialogue between the two. He also asserts that the extensive main areas of the earth, the continents, inasmuch they show differences regarding their natural disposition, correspondingly have brought about different "re-actions" and "re-sponses" of the human mind (P. 65).

Nichols (1995) Philosophical Cultural Differences chart, the only written document(unpublished) that we have seen from him so far, from a hand-out acquired in a workshop that that he presented, summarizes aspects that are bases of understanding theory and culture and as a means to conceptualizing Philosophical cultural differences from a global perspective. However Beck, (2002), and Marimba (1994) both provide a definitive description of the differences which shape today's worldview, its conflicts, and constraints.

Adapted from a workshop Hand-out by Edwin Nichols 1995 (unpublished source). Explaining further about the contrasting cultural differences, Beck, (2002) points out more definitively what Nichols's chart represents in summary, when he describes the consciousness differences the following, given the geographical-climate conditions of each continent and its people:

> *Thus, Africa invites people to live immediately out of nature to choose the "vital identification" with nature as their way of life; the continent of Asia, however, rather provokes an "intellectual withdrawal," a way of life shaped by introverted "spiritually keeping distance" (and "con-fronting") against nature by balancing calmness.*

Table 1.1. Philosophical Cultural Differences

Axiology	Epistemology	Logic	Process	Eurocentric
The highest value lies in the object or in the acquisition of things	Cognitive One knows through counting and measurement	Dichotomous Either/Or	All sets are repeatable	Occidental
The highest value lies in the interpersonal relationship	Effective One knows through symbolic imagery rhythm	Diunital The union of the opposites	Ntuology All sets are interrelated through human and spiritual network	Afrocentric Holistic and dynamic-creative sense
The highest values lies in the cohesion of the group	Conative One knows through striving towards the transcendence	Nyaya The objective world is conceived independent of thought & mind	Cosmology All sets are independently interrelated in the harmony of the universe	Asian centric Harmony and unity of Being

On the other hand, given the geographical and climate conditions, European's consciousness primarily inclines to differentiate and to structure reality rationally; whereby there is the typical tendency of setting demarcations and reaching articulating clarity. Thus,

> The more intuitive disposition of the African and African and Asian consciousness seems to have a more immediate and original relationship to reality; the European disposition, the stronger inclination to rational differentiation, demands more clearly and objectification which puts the empirical reality at a distance, a reflection turned outside.

This view confirms our assertion that, regarding the "seemingly," "resistance" or "ignorance" of western ways of thinking and education whether is in terms identity development, science or preventive care as far as medicine is concerned by African and African Americans. Beck (2002) continues further to assert that, the immediate-intuitive Afro-Asiatic and abstract-rational European disposition appear to form a contrary opposition. He also suggests that the African mode of intuition and Asiatic one do have a sub-contrary opposition. He stresses that; the differently accentuated structures of consciousness all over the continents could stimulate and complete one another through intercultural encounter, would promote and enrich the spiritual life of mankind in a "holistic" dynamic-creative sense.

According to Beck's description, the European consciousness due to its rational differentiation and distinction of partial aspects tendency, it abstractly picks out for itself, therefore, gaining fixing and objectivating distance against the unity offered by the experience of concrete connection of life and "Being." In this respect, the European unity of "Being" consciousness distinguishes and accentuates the plurality of the entities. On the contrary, the Afro-asiatic consciousness has a more original and powerful connection of all there is, which proclaims and stresses within the plurality of the entities the coherence and the unity of Being, which lays the foundation for the entities. This affirms why it is necessary to explore the relationship to nature and to man (Ntu—based on belief that, I am because we are). Thus, understanding the differences between various orientation as Beck (2002) points out describing Eurocentric perspective:

The relationship to nature in the occident, especially since modern times, typically is marked by the intention of the quantifying natural science and technology. Science according to its modern understanding, has to analyze the empirical connection of reality rationally, i.e. the immediately given "unity of experience "has to be resolved into its components. These components have to be picked out, in order to construct out of them, according to mathematical possibilities, in a technical-creative way, new complex unities which serve the human intentions better than did the structures of reality as given by nature.

It is evident that this consciousness is directly in opposition with African psyche and thus, since it has been imposed onto African Americans through socialization as well as to Africans through slavery on the latter and colonialism as well as neo-colonialism. Thus, it brings major constraint in an attempt to return to the original consciousness for both Africans, and African Americans. It makes it a double burden for African Americans or an Africans who has been Europeanized through education and socialization to deal with both European and Afro-asiatic consciousness, which creates a sort of schizophrenia that affects their trust, which is a basic need to human kind. It also impacts their world view in a pathological perspective that is contradictory to their psyche and the way they view identity and life in general.

An example given by Beck explains the Eurocentric or Occidental approach to identity and science of medicine causes the mistrust and distrust for African and African Americans:

The European-occidental approach of the science of medicine is different from the Afro-asiatic tradition in a culturally specific way. If there seems to be , for example, a disease of the liver or of the heart, the Western science of medicine primarily pays attention to the physical organ at question; it tries by analysis of the causes to determine the single elements of the defective structure and function, in order to put them into another, more desirable proportion, influencing it by drugs or attacking it surgically, i.e. through a rationally planned measure centered on the organ. In occidental culture, mind aims at confronting the contents of experience through active determination and alteration, i.e. through destroying the given structures of the physical and mental world until they are reduced to their elements, and out of these constructing new structures which correspond to man's very purpose (P. 69).

As Beck puts it, by objectification and domination of the world, obviously the freedom and all determining power and glorious mastership of mind is to be experienced and actively more and more actualized. This approach,

"constitutes the world as an object and therefore it can be determined and dominated which leads to "man aiming at his self-constitution as determining and dominating subject (P. 69)."

Beck's example of occidental approach to science results to contradictions for African and African Americans in conceptualizing identity that is positive and centered in Afrocentric world view. As beck again points, An African doctor does not see the cause primarily the organ itself," in order to fix it by analysis of factors" as in like the European way, rather, he understands the disease" holistically" as decrease in the vital force of the whole organism, wherein the affected organ participates in a special manner" whereby special force steadily flows into the organism from the spiritual-divine source of life which is immanent to the organism. The occidental culture thus, has created a Dis-equilibrium in the way most people view the world and it affects all aspects life, environmentally, technological which impacts negatively in human Psyche which results in arresting creativity and vital force, in economic, social, educational, political, and psychological. Mutisya and Ross (2006) points out that:

Afrocentricity is based on Afrology orAfricalogy which is the study of concepts, issues, and behaviors with particular bases in the African world, Diaspora and continental (Asante, 1988). The Afrocentric enterprise is framed by cosmological, epistemological, axiological, and aesthetic issues, of which the method of inquiry pursues a world voice distinctly African-centered in relationship to external phenomena on how we gather the meaning out of Africa or existence Asante (1990, P. 8). Afrocentric Paradigm is an abstraction based on societies indigenous to African continent prior to colonial rule (Mazrui, 1994). The African worldview (and African Science/Psychology within it) constitutes the only conceptual framework for general valid and reliable knowledge regarding the psychological functioning and behaviors of all African/Black People (Kambon, 1992).

They further content that Afrocentricity has been conceptualized as having several dimensions. For example, Asante (1994) notes that Afrocentric study is an orientation to data and facts that includes location, place, orientation, and perspective. In the construction of an Afrocentric scale, Kambon (1992) discusses four competencies: (1) awareness/recognition of a collective African identity and heritage, (2) general ideology and activity priorities placed on African survival and liberation, (3) specific activity (such as self-knowledge, African-centered values, etc.), and (4) a posture of resolute resistance toward anti-African forces and threats to African Diaspora survival. Grills & Longshore (1996) suggest that the seven principles of *Nguzo Saba* could be the basis of a simpler yet more comprehensive Afrocentric scale. Our own conceptualization involves centeredness in African culture and experience, symbols (symbols of African identity, philosophy, language, and culture), the hierarchical orientation of life (adult orientation), twiness of gender (equality of men and women and harmony between genders), universality and African Diaspora recognition (the recognition that although Africans have been scattered throughout the world, their culture and identity are still African), scholarship and research. As a concept, Afrocentricity can aid Africans to revitalize their cultural identity. Because of the negative impact of colonization, African identity revitalization seems to be necessary, especially for Africans who are no longer living in Africa. Afrocentricity may assist individuals of African descent to have a better appraisal of their culture and its values.

Racial socialization has been researched in the African American community (Taylor, Chatters, Tucker, & Lewis, 1991). Studies indicate that African American parents play a pivotal role in socializing children, helping them to understand norms, roles, statuses, and expectations of the larger society (Taylor et al., 1991). Parental socialization is but one of the many types of socialization agents. Gender role socialization and sexual orientation are modes of socialization that play a large role in children's identity. Other socialization agents may include schools, religion, peers, media, and others. Racial socialization in the African American community attempts to prepare black children for the realities of being African American in America. Limited studies have noted that about one-third of African American parents refused to discuss racial socialization messages with their children (Taylor et al., 1991).

Racial socialization encourages the teaching of cultural pride and preparation for racial discrimination to families (Boykin & Toms, 1985; Stevenson, Reed & Bodison, 1996). It is an important aspect of raising children. However, it may be quite difficult for African American parents to provide their children with positive group and self-identity since they are likely to face discrimination and prejudices from the larger society (Billingsley, 1992) in Mutisya and Ross in Black Studies Handbook (2006). Therefore, the strategies in Developing Conceptual Framework on Identity Development that we propose in this chapter include incorporating the theoretical background that we have developed thus far as well as paying attention to the following steps and that delineate the concepts and approach. We strongly believe that a conscious approach to dialogue is very crucial because it involves experiential learning and it is a transforming process.

WHY A CONCEPTUAL FRAMEWORK?

Richard (1993) asserts that successful intercultural communication and interaction does not usually occur by chance. Rather, it is the result of exchanges and behavior on the part of the persons who not only desire favorable results but have the skills necessary for generating and supporting positive outcomes. These skills may be yours-now or later-but, for success, a planned framework for their development is essential

- Conceptual Framework is a "Consciously organized arrangements of related information that, because we are aware of them, influence our actions.
- The degree to which we understand our own frameworks and the frameworks of others is often the degree to which we achieve unthreatened and successful human interactions.
- Our own personal frameworks are often determined by our cultures and to understand the significance of this observation, we must have an understanding of culture in general because we all view our world thorough culturally influenced frameworks that often collide with the different frameworks of others, which creates a conflict and thus we feel threatened.

January 18, 2000, at the Midwinter Meeting of the American Library Association in San Antonio, Texas defined information literacy this way:

Information literacy is a set of abilities requiring individuals to "recognize when information is needed and have the ability to locate, evaluate, and use effectively the needed information." Information literacy also is increasingly important in the contemporary environment of rapid technological change and proliferating information resources. Information literacy forms the basis for lifelong learning. It is common to all disciplines, to all learning environments, and to all levels of education. It enables learners to master content and extend their investigations, become more self-directed, and assume greater control over their own learning.

Therefore, we believe a culturally responsive conceptual framework should be composed of the following components that would be helpful in revitalizing African American cultural identity that transcends marginalization as a result of hegemony. The next step would involve developing an individual and collective Philosophical orientation and conceptualized from theory as we have discussed earlier. The next step would involve Affirming and Valuing my Diversity and understanding the Confluence between Diversity and Character. The Third step include developing an understanding of Intra-cultural Awareness: which establishes the meaning of "Who Am I?" and "What am I" for African American, White, Native American Latino/ Hispanic, and Asian American, and Inter-cultural Awareness—which explores the myths and facts that have distorted the identity development process in socialization. The next and the fourth step would be to develop awareness on Cross-cultural Awareness and the role of language in developing identity. Specifically, for African American, very little is discussed regarding the cross-cultural gap that exists between Africans and African Americans, whereby language and culture were the first aspects to be stripped off from which led to misconceptions of the meaning of belonging and self affirmation.

The fifth step is to establish awareness of how gender, age and sexual orientation, and physical abilities impact ones identity and avoid stereotypes that characterize African American culture as far as these. The last step we suggest is developing awareness on the shared American Culture from individual and collective perspectives. The framework should be guided by a critical conscious approach to dialogue (Concientizacao) as developed by (Freire, 94, and smith, 78), incorporated with Critical Pedagogy theories as part of strategies, which include concientizacao process questions. Concientizacao process questions involve helping participants in the dialogue identify and eradicate the contradictions in life that impact the individuals in an oppressive situation, in this respect for African Americans in their society, the impact on Cultural Identity, Politically, Socially, Economically, and Educational Perspectives; and how these Contradictions Affect Individuals Psychologically.

REFERENCES

Beck. H. Europe-Africa-Asia: The Creative Proportion between the World Cultures. Presby, G., Smith, D., Abuya, P., and Nyarwath, O. (2002). Thought and Practice in African Philosophy. Nairobi: Konrad Adenauer Foundation.

Banks, J.A. (2000). Cultural Diversity and Education: Foundations, Curriculum and Teaching, (Fourth edition). Boston: Allyn and Bacon.

Banks, J.A. (1993). Multicultural Education for Young Children: Racial and Ethnic Attitudes and their Modification. In B. Spodek (Ed.), Handbook of research on the education of young children (pp. 236–250). New York: Macmillan.

Banks, J.A. (2001). Cultural diversity and education: Foundations, curriculum, and, teaching (4th Ed.). Boston: Allyn and Bacon.

Bauer, A.M., and Shea, T.M. (Parents and Schools: Creating a Successful Partnership for Students with Special Needs.

Becher, R. M. (1984, January). *Parent Involvement: A Review of Research and Principles of Successful Practice.* Washington, D.C.: National Institute of Education.

Becher, R. M. (1984, January). *Parent Involvement: A Review of Research and Principles of Successful Practice.* Washington, D.C.: National Institute of Education.

Bermudez A., & Padron, Y. N. (1987). "Integrating Parental Education into Teacher Training Programs," *Journal of Educational Equity and Leadership*, 7(4), 23 5–244.

Chomsky on MisEducation. Lanham: Rowman & Littlefield Publishers.

Cotton, K., and Savard, W. G. Parent Involvement in Instruction, K-12: Research Synthesis. Portland, OR: Northwest Regional Educational Laboratory, 1982. (ED 235–397). http://www.nwrel.org/scpd/sirs/3/cu6.html

Delpit, L. (1995). Other people's children: Cultural conflict in the classroom. New York: The New Press.

Espinoza-Herold, M. (2003). Issues in Latino Education: Race, School Culture, and Politics of Academic Success. Boston: Pearson education Group, Inc.

Freire, Paulo (1994). The Pedagogy of hope: Reviving Pedagogy of the oppressed. New York: Continuum publishing Group.

Jedlicka, D. (2005). Ethnicity, Society and the Individual. National Social Science Press.

Kohl, A. (1994)." I won't Learn from You": and Other Thoughts on Creative Maladjustment. New York: New York Press.

Marshall, P. L. (2002). Cultural diversity in our schools. Belmont: Wadsworth Publishing Co. (ISBN# 0534511247X).

McLaren, P. (1998). Life in schools: An introduction to critical pedagogy in the foundations of education (3rd Ed.). New York: Longman.

National Coalition for African American Parent Involvement in Education (2007); www.ncaapie.org

Oliver, Bill (1999). Parent To Parent: Keeping Healthy Families Healthy. Marietta, GA: The Passage Group program workbook. Website: www.nsspress.com

Richard, B.V. (1993). "Developing Intercultural Communication Skills. Malabu Books.

Smith, William (1978). Meaning of Concientizacao: the Goal of Paulo Freire. Amherst: University of Massachusetts-Center for international Studies.

Tatum, B. (1999). (2nd Edition).Why are all the black kids sitting together in the Cafeteria? And other Conversations about Race. New York: Basic Books.

Wathiong'o Ngugi A. Decolonizing the Mind: The Politics of Language in African Literature, 1986).

Wink, J. (2005). Critical Pedagogy: Notes from Real World (3rd Ed.) Boston: Pearson Education, Inc.

Woodson, Carter G. (1992). The MisEducation of the Negro. Washington: Associated Publishers.

Chapter Two

Things Fall Apart: African American Families in New Orleans Responding to Hurricane Katrina

Jonathan N. Livingston, Harriette McAdoo,
George Cliette, and Jennyfer Holley

"Nothing will ever be the same."

A 35-year-old Homeless Black Male Laborer

ABSTRACT

Given the events of the past 2 years and the catastrophic impact of Hurricane Katrina upon the Gulf Coast and the families that call this area home, there is a need to better understand how this environmental tragedy has disrupted the lives of groups already politically and economically marginalized and understand how these changes have affected the lives of children. The present chapter will address the unique history, culture, and family life of African Americans in New Orleans as well as the challenges these families face as their entire community is currently in influx. Researchers will seek to ascertain, through interviews and qualitative analysis, not only the aftermath of this disaster on the families and children impacted by Hurricane Katrina but also how we as social scientists and human service professionals can assist in helping them rebuild their families and lives. The interviews were conducted over a 4-day period. Participants' responses were recorded and thematic content analysis was employed to elucidate consistent and salient themes across the data. Recorded interviews and pictorials were used to bring clarity to the impact that Hurricane Katrina had upon families in the Gulf area. Throughout the interviews, consistent themes regarding a need for housing, schools, employment, and the influence of racism in the decisions to provide resources and services to families emerged.

This chapter is composed of responses from semi-structured interviews and informal stakeholder interviews conducted nine months after Hurricane Katrina. In an effort to better understand the impact of Katrina, researchers interviewed individuals and families who had faced the devastation of Katrina as well as the flooding which occurred after the levees broke. We found that the major impact of the hurricane was, and still is, the continuing stress that has been placed upon the people and families of New Orleans. Although both Whites and Blacks were impacted by the hurricane, a disportionate number of Black citizens were affected. This is evident in the number of African Americans standing in water and living on bridges as was captured during the aftermath by the media. Americans trying to make sense of the events since Katrina have been astonished and amazed by the lack of responsiveness on the part of the federal government. According to Lowery (2006), this was more than just racism; it was plain incompetence, classism, and environmental irresponsibility. Thousands of low-income African Americans were uprooted from their homes like "so called" "refugees," a phrase coined by insensitive media, and have moved to Houston, Atlanta, Shreveport, and cities throughout Tennessee, South Carolina, Georgia, and North Carolina. As we approach the one year anniversary of Hurricane Katrina, many families are likely to re-experience feelings of loss as well as emotional and physical distress associated with this catastrophic event no matter where they reside (Foster, 2006). Currently, there are still inadequate mental health services to deal with the emotional feelings and physical distress experienced by individuals and families of Katrina. For families in New Orleans, their world has fallen apart and critical pieces of their lives are still missing.

THE IMPACT OF STRESS

On all economic levels, the stress of living through a hurricane has left a serious impact on all residents. A city rich on history and tradition and known for its diverse cultures has experienced an event which will change its complexity and complexion forever. Simply listening to the stories of the residents, one will see that there are definite signs of stress present among families. Given the loss of family and homes, depression, drug use, and suicide have increased. Suicide rates in New Orleans have almost tripled in the eleven months since the storm (Foster, 2006). The deputy coroner, who handles psychiatric cases, has stated that the annual suicide rate was about nine per 100,000 residents before the hurricane. It has now increased to more than 26 per 100,000 residents. Experts blame an epidemic of depression and post-traumatic stress on this increase. This epidemic has been found, not only among poor, but among all socioeconomic levels. Law enforcement officers are now answering more calls for domestic abuse, fights, drug related acts, and drunkenness. In addition, over the past year, there has been a substantial increase in homicides related to drugs in poor neighborhoods of central New Orleans. The legal system is also in disarray (Saulny, 2006). After a rash of violent events in the early summer, the Mayor asked the Governor to send in National Guard troops to help the city get through the myriad of social and economic challenges created by Katrina.

THE STATE OF NEW ORLEANS TODAY

Racism remains one of the continuing tragedies of Hurricane Katrina. Resolving sensitive racial and social questions are central to any effort in rebuilding and recovering after the hurricane (Ououssoff, 2006). The racial makeup of the city has changed. The Black population decreased from 37% to now 22%. The proportion of White individuals grew from 59% to now 73% of the population. The median income was $3,654 and rose to $43,447, due mainly to the displacement of poorer Black residents (Time, 2006).

The element of race became obvious in the election results. The altered demographics made a difference in the campaign and the election (Nossiter, 2006). Four out of five Blacks voted for the Black candidate, Ray Nagin, and four out of five Whites voted for his White opponent, Mitch Landrieu (Roberts, 2006; Robinson, 2006). Although displaced, more Blacks than expected went to the polls. Election Day was like a family reunion with music blaring as neighbors saw each other for the first time since the storm (Rudd, 2006). They insured that they had a "chocolate mayor." Often lacking the money to rebuild, they will likely remain in scattered sites, even though these families have roots that go back for over a century.

To get a perspective on the situation, one must look first at the situation of New Orleans in general. The New York Times presented Fellowes, Katz, Liu, and Holmes (2006) who surveyed the situation in New Orleans: before Katrina, six months later, and a year after the hurricane and floods. Despite the $2 billon in reconstruction aid for the victims, a significant amount of money has been lost to "scams, schemes, and bureaucratic bungles." The major institutions of New Orleans are not fully functioning, and many of the public services have not been restored. Social service agencies in the areas hardest hit are either nonexistent or barely functioning out of makeshift offices, which are unable to handle the increased demand. Neely Kennedy, the state treasurer of Louisiana, has gone on record saying that despite the spicy and colorful ethical standards of government that existed in New Orleans, they must have zero tolerance for the waste or theft of this money from the federal government (Kennedy 2006). The fact that the treasurer has to put this statement in the New York Times speaks volumes about the pressures city officials face when allocating resources and adequately monitoring expenditures.

When one takes a look at the infrastructure of New Orleans, only 50% of the hospitals are open. Only18–25% of schools have opened as of Fall 2006. Only 22% of the child care centers are open in the city. Although the city of New Orleans provided free bus service for many returning since the hurricane, currently only 17% of the commercial buses were operational. Forty-six percent of public libraries were opened in the city (Fellowes, et al, 2006). The adults who are still displaced by Hurricane Katrina represent 24.9% of the population. The unemployment rates are 6.4% in a labor force of 404,498 in the metropolitan area. The labor force that is still displaced by Hurricane Katrina equals 309,000 individuals (Fellowes, et al, 2006). As developers and contractors work to restore this great city, there are hard choices to be made about how to rebuild a low-lying city with enormous tracts of uninhabitable housing (Jet, 2006).

FAMILIES

Less than 50% of the 455,000 pre-Katrina New Orleans residents have returned. Those who have returned stay wherever they can find room (Roberts, 2006). The traditional extended family arrangements mean that family members try to stay together. But the extended time has made familial relationships more difficult. The strain of having so many family members together causes severe stress on all involved. The family member providing shelter feels there is no other way. Social class becomes a dominant factor in even greater form when they begin to plan the rebuilding of the different areas. After Katrina, poorer residents were standing on their roofs waiting for rescuers to take them to the Superdome while other evacuees who could afford to leave were driving out of town to hotels or places with other family members. Now officials are trying to determine which neighborhoods will be rebuilt or repaired and which will be abandoned or reverted to swampland (Rivlin, 2006). As one walks through the areas hardest hit by the hurricane and floods, the sounds of some neighborhoods are of hammers and nail guns while the sounds of others are of dead silence. Areas such as the Ninth Ward are barren and lifeless. Houses have been removed completely from their lots either by the force of the water released from the levee or by cleanup efforts. An area once characterized by an abundance of children and older residents sitting on their porches now resembles a ghost town.

There are disparities between the rich and poor as African Americans move into the planning stages of rebuilding their communities. With the loss of neighborhood leadership, each neighborhood has to be reorganized and must decide on its own rules. People without advanced education and experience with the government are not as organized as the richer ones are. Two examples are shown in Eastover, a gated community that is home to many wealthy Black persons, and Lower Ninth Ward, where many became isolated on their roofs. More than half of those in the Ninth Ward owned their own homes, but they were not organized into a homeowners association. Their homes averaged about $70,000. There are no FEMA trailers because they are still without gas and drinkable water. However, those in Eastover were organized before the floods, and their homes averaged from $400,000 to over one million dollars. They were able to hire professionals to help them get their plans together to rebuild (Rivlin, 2006).

Although the Army core of engineers have accepted blame for the flooding, many believe that the levees were never a sound, complete system (Schwartz a., 2006). Discussions with many of the residents who experienced Betsy in 1965, suggested that race and class had always had an intimate relationship with the levee system and how the waters flowed in New Orleans. Efforts to explain what happened the summer of 2005 are riddled in myth and conjecture. The major myth is that those in the Lower Ninth area are more prone to flooding than the other areas because the land is lower. A careful review of the geography of New Orleans suggests that the Lower Ninth is "two or three feet higher" than the Lakeview neighborhood and the western side of Jefferson Parish. It has also been said that a good flood-control system will help the entire city, and that is what is needed (Schwartz b., 2006). However, given the socio-political context of New Orleans and the divide between the "haves" and the "have-nots," no system will be devoid of the influence of race and class.

SCHOOLS

The lack of a fully operating school system is a problem that has hurt many families. Marian Wright Edelman has said that the youngest victims of the storm are still suffering. She also states that we have to give the children something enriching, caring, and safe (Edelman, 2006). These children need help and have so many unmet needs. To address the unmet needs of Katrina's children, the Children's Defense Fund (CDF) opened 13 Freedom Schools this summer. Children are taught by high school and college interns, who serve as mentors. CDF provides the training and curriculum for the schools. The community groups there work to raise money to keep them running. The schools serve 75–100 children. The children are seeing the adults go through so much stress that they do not understand what is going on. They need to be able to be given hope. The needs of the children are massive, and CDF hopes to have the schools open year round.

METHODS

In an effort to gain a clear picture of the impact of Hurricane Katrina upon children and families, researchers from North Carolina Central University visited areas most devastated by the hurricane during the months of May and August. Through five structured interviews and discussions with key informants, public officials, community activists, and business owners; researchers gained valuable insights on the immediate needs of families in New Orleans. The five structured interviews were conducted over a four day period. Participants' responses were recorded, and photographs were also taken to humanize our efforts and bring clarity to the impact that Hurricane Katrina had upon families in the Gulf area. Participants were provided a consent form for both the audio taped interview and for photographs taken. And each person was compensated $25.00 for participating in the study.

PARTICIPANTS

The participants who were interviewed were middle and lower income African Americans who had returned to New Orleans. Criteria for participation in the study included being at least age 18 and taking care of children. Key informants from the New Orleans area were contacted, and they aided the researchers in identifying families who had resettled in New Orleans since the hurricane. Five families were contacted and interviewed. The participants ranged from 19 to 60 years of age. Some were employed in the service industry, and some of the younger families were on public assistance. Prior to Katrina, one of the participants was a school teacher and the other was a community activist. Even though most of the participants were unemployed, they did work prior to Katrina. At the time of the interview, many resided in what was known as the Ninth Ward and East New Orleans, areas most devastated by the hurricane. Each of the participants either had children or grandchildren of whom they were the primary caretaker. Participants indicated that some of their older children were still displaced by the storm in cities such as Houston and Atlanta. However, most had at least made contact with their parents to assure their safety. The participants' income ranged from $15,000 to $45,000. Most were high school graduates and were natives of New Orleans. Two trained interviewers conducted the interviews. Both researchers were of the same race as the participants. A semi-structured interview protocol was used in the study. A series of questions regarding the impact of Hurricane Katrina and resources needed were provided. All interviews were audio taped and later transcribed verbatim for analysis.

DATA REDUCTION

To better understand the experiences of the families of New Orleans, a phenomenological approach was employed. The phenomenological approach seeks to understand the meaning of the lived experience of a specific individual or group of people. This process is done to capture the essence of the meaning of the lived experience. According to Van Manen in 1982, the essence is a description of the phenomenon that lays out the framework of the lived experience so that it becomes accessible and meaningful to the researcher and the reader. Thus, the phenomenological approach was used in the present study.

To assess or investigate the experiences of families and children who were impacted by the hurricane, a series of questions were asked of respondents. *"How has Hurricane Katrina impacted your family?" "How have the children adjusted to relocation?" "What were some of the significant challenges for your children?" "What resources are you and your family members most in need of as you seek to restore your family?"* Responses to these questions and probes (e.g. Could you explain more?) were analyzed. Thematic content analysis was employed to elucidate consistent and salient themes across the data. Once data was transcribed by researchers, salient themes were derived. Participant responses were compared to assess any consistent themes among participants.

RESULTS

Several themes emerged from the participants. Housing, unemployment, lack of schools, structural racism, and governmental neglect were salient themes gleaned from the data.

HOUSING

Access to affordable housing still remains a key issue for many of the residents of New Orleans. Many of the residents who decided to stay are struggling to rebuild homes that are not habitable. Those who are slowly returning are returning to communities that have been decimated by a deluge of water and sewage. Many of the families find themselves living two to three families per house in areas where rent has increased by almost 100%. This situation presents a considerable amount of stress for homeowners of the Ninth Ward, who lost more than just a house. They lost a sense of community, and this is reflected as one participant indicated:

> "[The Lower Ninth Ward before Katrina] *It was beautiful because most of the people down there . . . I would say it was 80–90% African American. Most of the people were homeowners. Even though they were real poor, a lot of people built their own houses. And my dad was a carpenter; my momma was a carpenter. So, we went up and down the block helping people build their houses. And so it was a very closely knitted community."*—58-year-old Muslim grandfather

Efforts by FEMA, in many instances, have been the sole responses to the need for housing. Pre-existing housing agencies are either not currently operating or are too poorly staffed to be functional to meet the needs of the people.

> *"Homes, they need homes. It's taken so long for those people to get these trailers . . . these people don't have nowhere to stay. And then half of them, their insurance fighting them to pay them their insurance. They can't even get their insurance for them to start over."* 34-year-old Black female

She went on further to suggest that, for homeowners, even attempts to try to secure housing were complicated by pre-existing archaic formulas denoting or ascribing need.

> *"They did but it was kind of hard. . . . Because you would think, by you having a home, you would get some help. But it wasn't, it was hard for me to get help . . . being that I had a home because it was like, "You can't get no Section 8 or apartment because you own your own home. And that was a hurtful thing. I couldn't even walk up and say I need a home."* 34-year-old Black female

Those who have decided to come back, come back to not only a city torn by politics and a natural disaster, but they come back to communities where memories of friends and families still linger among decay, blight, and the suffocating smell of mildew.

> *"Why did I come back? Because, I was homesick. It was . . . I mean . . . I felt trapped in Texas 'cause I couldn't do nothing . . . only thing I could do was just sit in the apartment 'cause I don't know nothing about Texas."* 34-year-old female

Although for many, coming home was painful. Home was all they knew, and it was better than living in a modern apartment in another city where they had no social, psychological, or emotional connections. The pain became more poignant as people came to realize that their neighborhood would never be the same. Many of the childhood memories had been erased and eradicated forever by the putrid floodwaters of Katrina.

"They just don't know how grateful I am. Just to have a roof . . . really it was like . . . this was just my house not my home . . . it never was my home. I never really looked at it as my home . . . it was my house . . . that's it. But those are 2 different things. You can have a house or you can have a home. I had a house to say I had a house but I never had a home." 34 year old Black female

Returning home for many, although bittersweet, gave some of them at least a familiarity and social connections that they were used to prior to Katrina.

EMPLOYMENT

Prior to Katrina, employment in New Orleans has primarily consisted of a tourist and service industry. Since the storm, many of the businesses which reside outside of the French Quarter are still not open. Thus, there has been a tremendous loss of jobs in Greater New Orleans. Moreover given the water damage to many of the civil service buildings, many city and government workers are unable to return to work. Most of the discussion regarding employment centered on the rebuilding of New Orleans. Discussions with key informants and community stakeholders suggest that the indigenous men were involved in the cleaning and rebuilding of New Orleans. On any given day, one could see crews of either European American, Latin American, or Mexican American laborers working to rebuild a city formally built by many African Americans. This makes one wonder why is this happening and how will it impact the vitality of African American families and communities in New Orleans.

". . . when I have a financial crisis, my daughter was a dentist and she was always willing to share her monies because she was making over $250,000.00 before the storm. But, I'm the kind of person that I don't like to ask anybody." 58-year-old Muslim grandfather

SCHOOLS

Prior to Hurricane Katrina, New Orleans schools, as well as many school districts in the state of Louisiana, had problems. Plagued by poor performance, high dropout rates, and poor pay for teachers, Louisiana schools have continued to be some of the worst schools in the country. Since Katrina, many of the schools have been closed. As we reach the first school year post-Katrina, only 15–20% of the students have returned. Many are returning to schools that are under-funded and teachers that are nonexistent. Therefore, a number of children who stayed in New Orleans or are returning are not enrolled in the schools. As one of the participants indicated:

> *"A lot of kids are not in school. I know a lot of kids that are not in school because of that. I know a lot of kids in the neighborhood. They're not going to school because of that [Hurricane Katrina]. Yep, and like when you try to register them for school, they ask you for a lot of things and you tell them they got messed up in the Hurricane."* 19-year-old Black mother of two

A significant barrier for many guardians and parents is that of establishing custody and providing proper information on the child prior to enrollment. School officials, even amidst the chaos and turmoil caused by Hurricane Katrina, still are demanding documentation from parents who have lost everything.

> *"Well, we can't do nothing for you." How could you deny a child an education because of something that's not their fault?" "I have a little cousin on that picture right there that I have custody of right there that I have to take care of and I can't get her into school. It's hard for me to get her into a school and that's hard to believe. Because, I mean, all the schools are full and they not taking children and I'm like how could you not take one child?"* 19-year-old Black mother of two

RACISM

In New Orleans and much of Louisiana, race, politics, and money have always been strange bedfellows. The influence of Spanish, French, Indian, and African culture has created a cultural and ethnic mixture which, in some instances, blurs the lines of class and caste. Although New Orleans is predominately African American, separate sects such as Creoles and Native Americans have coexisted and contributed to the culture of New Orleans. In talking with participants about the influence of race, many seemed reluctant to discuss the racial significance of Katrina. And whether it is reflective of the intimate and unique relationships that the original Africans via Haiti and West Indies and French colonists shared in New Orleans or the current context of political correctness dominating much of the discussion about race, there was a resistance to discuss Katrina and the government's lack of response in terms of race. When key informants and stakeholders were asked about the statements that Mayor Ray Nagin had made suggesting that New Orleans would continue to be a *"chocolate city,"* many seemed more concerned about housing and their next meal than talking about racism and their social location. However when the conversation centered around the cleanup and the redevelopment of New Orleans, race became a salient theme and was reflected in a statement made by an 18-year old service worker on Bourbon Street:

"White people don't spend money on Black people."

In our informal discussions with elders who had experienced both Betsy and Katrina, race and economics were said to have played a significant role in the politics and the management of the levee systems in New Orleans. One of the elderly women in the community suggested that the levees were deliberately destroyed during Betsy in 1965 in order to protect the White community. She indicated that the Ninth Ward and many of the Black communities were flooded, and a number of lives were lost in order to save property. The look on her face was one of assurance and a keen understanding of the racial dynamic in a city she had called home for more than 70 years. Her story and the story of a number of older Black and White New Orleans residents were consistent concerning the floods during Betsy. Without the coverage of CNN, Fox, and other major television stations, one could see the destruction and loss of lives they spoke of in 1965.

Community Responsiveness

In the wake of a natural disaster, the world often watches the terror-stricken community come together to help each other. One prime example is the event of 9/11. America, along with the world, witnessed the surrounding communities support one another as bodies continued to be recovered and the number of missing people continued to rise. At the beginning, America was not seeing a lot of the camaraderie and "brotherly love" amongst the citizens of New Orleans. Most of the stories and depictions consisted of violence and "looting" and not of communities banding together to help one another through this horrific crisis. Some looting did occur as well as some violence. There was also evidence of discrimination represented by events such as the armed blockade guarding entrance from the Mississippi River Bridge into Gretna, LA. Many communities were not readily open or hospitable to evacuees from the flooding. Some Americans were blatantly callous and perfidious in their actions and comments. According to one elderly White male in Mississippi, *"They're (evacuees of New Orleans stranded on the Mississippi River Bridge) animals. You should cut the bridge off and let them kill themselves."* However, stories of brotherliness were, and continue to be, out there. According to one citizen, there was no other choice but to count on each other.

"We had to come together. We had to stick together because that was a time to stick together. We all in the same boat. None of us don't have nothing. We don't know if we are coming or going. Where are we goin'?" 19-year-old Black mother of two

Stranded on bridges and roofs and in trees and vehicles, the citizens, including the children, of New Orleans depended on the support of one another for days. Citizens remembered hearing chaotic screams during the night from men, women, and children needing help in getting off rooftops and navigating or swimming through the flood waters.

Partly due to the acute conditions of the city, people were not being rescued in a timely fashion from horrific situations. With inadequate resources, many citizens of New Orleans had to lean on their families, friends, and strangers for support. Whether in the Superdome, Convention Center, an attic, a rooftop, or on a bridge, the people of New Orleans found themselves encouraging and comforting one another in the very midst of disaster. Children were scared, hungry, and limited in their capacity to understand the gravity of the dire situation that surrounded them. The survivors of Katrina did what they could to comfort the elderly and the children. There are many stories of citizens working to keep each other calm and keep children encouraged. Some heroic citizens banded together to help one another survive physically and emotionally.

"We had a couple of guys that were really trying to help. Trying to help the kids and trying to help organize everything and they maybe had at least about 7 bottles of water where they tried to help by dividing it up by all the kids and older people just trying to put dabs in their mouth, you know, just trying to make sure that their tongues were wet, you know what I mean. And stuff like that. You know that a couple of guys like that was real helpful." 19-year-old Black mother of two

According to some of the local witnesses, citizens whose homes were not damaged were kept from helping their fellow citizens whose lives had been ravaged by the flooding. Many people with resources who wanted to stay and help were forced to leave and told their help was not needed, according to Malik Rahim, a former member of the Black Panther Party. Some agencies were also kept from helping the citizens of New Orleans. In the beginning of this catastrophe, The Red Cross was not granted permission to enter into the city. The reason given for this denial was due to its being a private agency. So in the crucial first days following the onslaught of Katrina, the citizens and children of New Orleans were largely dependent upon one another for comfort and survival. Afterwards, individuals, volunteers, churches, schools, and agencies provided food, clothing, donations, and shelter to the evacuees of the city. Volunteers at Saint Augustine's church fed 1000 families a week after Katrina.

According to one citizen, *"Well, they [Catholic charities] gave us food. They gave us clothes. They gave us cases of, you know, like 12 waters, cold drinks. They gave us enough food for at least 2 or 3 days and clothing."* 36-year-old Black female

Different organizations are coming up with ways to help restore the city, not just residentially, but culturally as well. For instance, the Ashe Cultural Arts Center accepts donations of musical instruments; Making It Happen is committed to revitalizing the cultural scene. There are groups committed to training individuals in stress management and crime prevention strategies. There are also individuals donating clothing and food still. Websites have been created to post information for those needing or offering assistance.

GOVERNMENTAL NEGLECT

Giving the litany of interviews, talk shows, and commentaries aired or published since the hurricane, one fact remains key. The government, at all levels, neglected to respond to the needs of people impacted by Katrina and in New Orleans, in particular. The slow cleanup and redevelopment effort in many of the low-income areas and the inability of FEMA to assist in finding housing for thousands of New Orleans suggest political apathy or benign neglect. This sentiment was echoed eloquently in a statement by one of the participants.

"To me, to be quite honest with you, President Bush—he's the worst President that we ever had. And if he wasn't so involved in Iraq, he could have taken care of this down here because a lot of people suffered-not only black people but white people too. But he's concerned with Iraq. And to that degree, he can't do what he was supposed to have done down here."—58-year-old Muslim grandfather

When asked about governmental sources and resources received since the hurricane, many participants became angered. Memories of sleeping in the superdome or convention center and witnessing dead bodies of those too familiar lie in the streets for days brought back memories many had tried to repress. While gathering herself from tears, one participant said, *"They didn't come back to bring us-we didn't receive water and food for four days. We didn't have no water or food. We had elderly that was dead on the bridge. Children dead on the bridge. With us it was like 400 people on the bridge. We was just there with dead bodies. With no help." "We need a new mayor-a new government. Somebody that's going to show that they gonna care for us."* 36-year-old female. As local, state, and federal governments struggled with how to respond and assist people and major news stations continued to feed and bathe in stories of race, sex, and pillage, the stories from participants shed a different light upon the people of New Orleans. When the government did not respond, people reached out to each other and began to work together. In contrary to the pictures painted by the media, they spoke of heroism, humanity, and collective survival.

> *"I mean people . . . they had this one lady that was 92 and she was like, "I came this far and they about to let this Hurricane kill me" . . . and her grandchildren put her in a child's swimming pool and dragged her to the supermarket in the water. And it just was horrible."* 19-year-old Black mother of two

> Amidst confusion, chaos, no telephones, and days without radio or television, many of the participants indicated there was nowhere to go for answers. *"It was a lack of communication . . . a big lack of communication. It's like, none of these people . . . there was no plan. There wasn't a plan. There was no evacuation plan. They have one now. But there was no plan at all."* 34-year-old Black female.

CONCLUSIONS

Whether it was race, class, or economics, thousands of children and families have been uprooted and removed from their homes since Katrina. Many of their parents were employees, homeowners, war veterans, and taxpayers. They were neither refugees nor derelicts; they were American citizens. Putting the pieces of their lives back together will require a collaborative effort among government at all levels, social and mental health services, as well as, the business and faith community. Although for many, redevelopment is of key importance to the economic survival of New Orleans. The emotional and psychological healing will require time, patience, and responsiveness by government which reflects benevolence, humanity, and compassion. As we approach a year since Hurricane Katrina and one walks through the Ninth Ward, East New Orleans, or Canal Street, the smell of mold, sewage, and trash lingers not to far behind that of death and blight. Although the people are slowly coming back one family at a time, the pain of memories of friends and family are etched throughout their faces. Looking into the eyes of many of the children, one easily sees that something is lost. Innocence and a belief in democracy and fairness or even a belief in a Higher Power has been replaced by an empty stare and a hardened posture, which suggests to anyone who navigates their path, that things have truly fallen apart.

RECOMMENDATIONS

1. There clearly is a need for affordable housing in the entire city of New Orleans. Participants indicated that housing has increased from 70–100%. Such an increase is counterproductive to rebuilding efforts in New Orleans given the high rate of unemployment.
2. Given the destruction of many of the industries in the area, New Orleans is primarily, purely a service economy. Moreover, the influx of Latin American immigrants has displaced many of the Black men who are skilled and unskilled laborers out of the workforce. Recently, New Orleans re-elected the mayor.
3. Many of the school-aged children were not able to attend school due to destruction to many of the school buildings and the displacement of school teachers. Also, many of the school children find themselves in home schools or reassigned to other school districts. There is a great need for schools, teachers, and other educational resources.
4. Mental health services and other social services are minimal or inadequate to address the needs of these families.
5. Leadership and support systems of many communities are displaced, and therefore, there is not adequate support to provide existing communities leadership.
6. Psychological services for children are needed with a particular emphasis on post-traumatic stress disorder, depression, anxiety, and adjustment disorder.
7. Social and psychological services for orphaned children are needed.

REFERENCES

Copeland, Larry. In Mississippi, Katrina recovery gaining stream. USA Today, July 25, 2006. 1A, 2A.

Drew, Christopher. Storm-Born Houston connection swells New Orleans drug trade. New York Times August 5, 2006.

Edelman, Marian Wright. Quoted in Lee, Trymaine. New Freedom Schools in New Orleans help Katrina youth. The Crisis. July/August 2006. 5–6.

Foster, Mary. Stress builds in N. Orleans 1 year after Katrina. Lansing State Journal. Aug. 11, 2006.

Fellowes, Matt, Katz, Bruce, Liu, Amy and Holmes, Nigel. The State of New Orleans: An Update. New York Times, July 5, 2006.

Jet. National Report. New Orleans mayor Ray Nagin sworn in a second term. June 20, 2006. 6–7.

Kennedy, John Neely. Lousiana's contract with America. New York Times, August 12, 2006, Section 3, 2.

Lowery, Joseph. Interviewed on CNN. Quoted by Rebecca Parker in Love first.

UUWorld. Summer 2006, 23–24.

Nossiter, Adam. Conservative White voters hold sway in an altered New Orleans electoral landscape. New York Times. April 7, 2006, 26.

Notebook. Time, June 19, 2006, p. 24.

Ouroussoff, Nicolai. In New Orleans, each resident is master of plan to rebuild. New York Times. Aug. 8, 2006. B1, B7.

Rivlin, Gary. In rebuilding as in the disaster, wealth and class help define New Orleans. April 25, 2006. A24.

Roberts, Michelle. Blacks backed Nagin in New Orleans race.Lansing State Journal. April 24, 2006. 4A.

Roberts, Michelle. Packed together after Katrina, families find benefits, challenges. Lansing State Journal, May 1, 2006. 8A.

Rudd, Shayna. In the Lower Ninth, a day of voting and reunions. New York Times. May 21, 2006. A24.

Saulny, Susan. New Orleans details steps to repair its legal system. New York Times. August 8, 2006. A12.

Schwartz, John. Army builders accept blame over flooding. New Orleans protection was "in Name Only." New York Times. June 2, 2006. A1, A16.

Schwartz, John. A scientist's book on Katrina draws fire at L.S.U. New York Times. May 30, 2006. A1, A4.

Schwartz, John. How low is the Lower 9th? Ward's fate may lie in the answer.

Chapter Three

Our Souls Look Back in Wonder: The Spirituality of African American Families Surviving Hurricane Katrina

Monica Terrell Leach, Pamela P. Martin,
Tuere A. Bowles, and Jocelyn DeVance Taliaferro

ACKNOWLEDGMENTS

We thank the resilient people of Slidell, Louisiana and the members of the Making It on Broken Pieces Project for their help with data collection. Correspondence should be addressed to Monica Terrell Leach, Department of Social Work, 106 Caldwell Hall, North Carolina State University, Raleigh, NC, 27695-8101. The first author can also be reached by electronic mail at monica_leach@ncsu.edu.

ABSTRACT

In 2005, the catastrophic impact of Hurricane Katrina dismantled families of various backgrounds in the Gulf Coast region. Using a qualitative approach in this chapter, we explored how religion and spirituality influenced the experiences of African American families living in Slidell, Louisiana in the aftermath of Katrina. We examined not only the aftermath of this disaster on the families, but also how African American families used faith-based social support networks as a resource in the midst of a natural disaster to rebuild their lives after such a traumatic environmental tragedy. This chapter concludes with implications for practice with African American families. Key terms: African American families, Hurricane Katrina, religion, and spirituality.

> *"If I never believed—and I always have—I definitely do now."—41-year-old mother of two*

When major disaster strikes any community, the majority of its residents are never fully prepared. People often speculate and seek God for answers, trying to understand the reasons *why* the catastrophe happened. Disasters generally have the greatest impact on vulnerable populations (e.g., racial minorities, renters, single headed households) due to their lack of human and financial resources needed to recover (Sanders, Bowie, & Bowie, 2003). Families with children are particularly vulnerable to disasters (Zakour & Harrell, 2003). When providing services to children, it is tremendously important to interact with them in the context of their family. Children are not the change agents in most families and therefore, the norms, activities, and behaviors of the family system directly affect the children and their ability to respond to crises. While children are resilient and have their own coping mechanisms, it must be acknowledged that the strategies used by adult family members will influence the child's ability to cope with the disaster. As such, familial responses to crisis are the focus of this chapter.

While many other areas such as New Orleans and the Mississippi Gulf Coast have received significant attention from scholars (Briggs, 2006; Rivera & Miller, 2007; Sharkey, 2007), areas like Slidell, Louisiana have largely been ignored even though Slidell is a city in St. Tammany Parish prominently situated between Mississippi and New Orleans. The I-10 twin-span bridge, which connects Slidell to New Orleans, was decimated in the storm leaving no connectivity to New Orleans from the north shore. Once the storm was over, Katrina's wrath seriously damaged over 4,000 St. Tammany parish homes with over 700 personal properties, houses and businesses totally destroyed in the City of Slidell (Louisiana Speaks, 2006).

The western eye wall of Hurricane Katrina hit Slidell located on the north shore of New Orleans with winds gusting over 125mph (Louisiana Speaks, 2006). Furthermore, Slidell is surrounded by bayous and lakes, making it particularly susceptible to flooding and rising water. While many other areas, such as New Orleans and Biloxi, received significant attention from researchers and the media, areas like Slidell have not been part of the public discourse.

REVIEW OF THE LITERATURE

Historically and presently, religion and spirituality represent an integral component of the personal identity of African Americans. In the review of the literature we define key terms and explicate three major areas: religious involvement of African Americans; positive outcomes of religion and spirituality; and, coping mechanisms of religion and spirituality. Religion refers to a form of worship that includes a system of attitudes, beliefs, and practices that is both personally held as well as advocated by an organization (Kyeremateng, 1998). Religion primary instructs individuals about moral values, and socializes them according to a particular unifying doctrine (Koenig, McCullough, & Larson, 2001; Mattis & Jagers, 2001; Pargament & Maton, 2000). In the midst of unexpected events, like natural disasters, religion provides a framework, which can be used to navigate unanticipated life experiences. Spirituality, on the other hand, refers to the transcendent, and often non-material/intangible aspects of human existence and awareness (Mattis, 1997; 2000). Both religion and spirituality instill a worldview that permeates the self and, in turn, provides an individual with a shared worldview in which s/he may interpret and interact with God, family members, and the wider society.

Previous studies have documented a substantial percentage of African Americans practice their faith through participating in organized religious activities as well as utilize spiritual practices (e.g., prayer, meditation, etc.) to comprehend their relationship to God. To illustrate, Gallop and Jones (2000) reported that approximately 80% of African Americans worship God in formal, organized settings. They also reported that 83% of African Americans believe religion can help solve many of the moral and social ills of today as compared to only 53% of Whites. In addition, approximately 54% of African Americans attend church weekly as compared to only 42% of Whites, and 78% African Americans claimed church membership as compared to only 68% of Whites. In another study, Taylor, Chatters, and Levin (2004) reexamined data from the General Social Survey wherein they found that close to 70% of African Americans indicated that they were both religious and spiritual. These same researchers using the National Survey of American Life reported that 80% of African Americans indicate religion and spirituality as extremely important in their daily lives (Taylor et al., 2004). The findings from these various national samples strongly indicate the centrality of religion and spirituality among a great number of African Americans.

Empirical studies suggest that religious involvement and spirituality may be a direct link to understanding positive psychological and health outcomes among African Americans. Ellison (1991; 1998) plus Ellison and Gay (1990), for example, using the National Survey of Black Americans found that participation in organizational (e.g., church attendance and church choir) and non-organizational religious activities (e.g., praying and viewing religious television) among adults is positively related to the overall life satisfaction, friendliness, self-esteem, and satisfaction with family life. Brown and Gary (as cited in Taylor et al., 2004) examined the relation between three indices of religiosity (i.e., denominational affiliation, church attendance, and overall religiosity) and negative health behaviors such as smoking and daily drinking among a community sample of African American males. Their results indicated that these indices of religiosity functioned as a strong preventive effect regarding male participation in these adverse health risk behaviors which medical research has noted may contribute potentially to several chronic diseases such as lung cancer, throat cancer, and liver disease. More recently, strong evidence from other empirical works suggests spirituality among diverse samples of African Americans is positively associated with healthy nutritional habits (Bowen-Reid & Smalls, 2004) and optimism (Mattis, Fontenot, & Hatcher-Kay, 2003).

In conceptualizing religious involvement and spirituality, an indirect mediational relation has been delineated by different scholars to explain coping and health outcomes (McNully, Livneh, & Wilson, 2004; Utsey, Bolden, Williams, Lee, Lanier et al., 2007). Additional support for a mediational link through different dimensions of religiousness and spirituality in understanding the direct relation between demographic factors and various social, cognitive, psycho-behavioral outcomes among African Americans is reflected in the relational framework by Mattis and Jagers (2001). Essentially, religion and spirituality represent complex functions that potentially influence the interpretation of daily experiences that socializes the different ways African Americans interact within and outside their community. Utsey and colleagues (2007) have demonstrated that spiritual well-being partially mediates culturally-specific practices and quality of life indicators such as environmental health, physical health, psychological health and social relationships.

Additionally, religion and spirituality have been described as coping mechanisms individuals entrust to handle unexpected adverse life circumstances. An emergent research literature on African American Hurricane Katrina survivors has begun to investigate the different coping strategies employed to sustain and protect them from unfavorable physical and mental health outcomes. For instance, elderly African American Katrina survivors discussed regular communication with a higher power, participation in non-organizational activities such as reading the Bible as well as involvement in stewardship activities that allowed them to help other individuals cope with the aftermath of the hurricane (Lawson & Thomas, 2007). The researchers of this qualitative study pointed to spirituality functioning as an emotional resilient factor that allowed participants to utilize this resource to interpret and respond to their social environment.

Within this context, it is expected that African Americans residents in Slidell, Louisiana, after surviving one of the most tremendous natural disasters in recent American history, would be impacted spiritually. This research was to determine how that impact, specifically the coping mechanisms, shaped their faith in God as they recovered from the disaster of Hurricane Katrina.

METHOD

Participants

Twelve African American Hurricane Katrina survivors (10 female, 2 male) participated in this study. The mean age of participants was 44 years-old although they ranged in age from 21 to 65 years. All of the participants were born in Louisiana and eight of the twelve were lifetime Slidell residents. Following Katrina, participants evacuated to Alabama, Mississippi, North Carolina, and Texas. In an effort to rebuild their lives in Slidell, participants in this study returned home three to eight months following their evacuation.

Levels of education for participants in this study spanned from grade school to college. Participants' occupations included administrators, technicians, contractors and retirees. The marital status included the following: three were single never married; one was divorced; and eight were married. All of the survivors had children; and, nine had children under the age of 18 living in the household. Finally, five of the Katrina survivors experienced Hurricane Betsy in 1965. (See Table 3.1 for demographic information on each participant.)

Procedures

Recruitment of participants. A purposive sample was selected for this study. Purposive sampling, also termed *purposeful* (Patton, 2002), aims to select "*information-rich cases* for study in depth" (p. 46). To obtain information-rich cases for this study, participants had to be African American adult residents of Slidell for at least one year prior to Katrina. Additionally, participants had to have returned to Slidell within twelve months following Katrina. Based on the aforementioned criteria, participants were identified via personal contact by the lead investigator with the assistance of faith communities in Slidell. To recruit participants, informational letters were distributed and announcements made at the churches. From the responses of interest shared by local pastors, the lead investigator contacted participants via telephone and/or e-mail to explain the purpose of the study, the study is completely voluntary, limited risks were anticipated, and confidentiality of responses was maintained.

Interviews. The primary method of collecting data for this study was through qualitative interviewing. Participants were interviewed face-to-face in their homes and places of worship ranging from one and one half hours to three hours in length. A semi-structured interview guide was employed in order to compare responses from participants, yet allow for probing questions.

Table 3.1. African American Katrina Survivors' Demographics

Pseudonym	Age	Marital Status	Children	Education	Years Lived in Slidell	Experienced Hurricane Betsy (1965)
Marilyn	65	Married	2	HS Diploma	65	Yes
Ellis	63	Married	3	HS Diploma	63	Yes
Vonda	61	Married	3	HS Diploma	61	Yes
Etta	48	Divorced	1	Some College	40	Yes
Jackie	43	Married	3	HS Diploma	43	Yes
Lynette	42	Single	2	Associates	42	No
Shannon	41	Married	2	Some College	9	No
Barbara	40	Married	3	Some College	40	No
Tony	40	Married	2	HS Diploma	6	No
Frances	37	Married	2	HS Diploma	6	No
Tracey	28	Single	1	Some College	28	No
Lauren	21	Single	1	GED/Grade School	21	No

Note: Pseudynoms were used to protect the confidentiality of the participants.

Areas explored in the interview included participants' experiences during and after Katrina, use of social support networks, and the role of one's faith during and following the natural disaster. Participants were assigned pseudonyms by the lead researcher to protect identities. Also follow-up interviews were conducted, as needed, via telephone to clarify or request additional information. Interviews were audio taped and transcribed. Transcripts of the interviews were then given to participants for corrections and additions.

Participant observations. The secondary method of collecting data for this study was participant observations. Bogdan and Biklen (2003) define participant observations as "an approach to qualitative research where the researcher spends prolonged periods of time in the subject's natural environment, unobtrusively collecting data. The researcher is simultaneously a participant and an observer" (p. 261). Thus, during the interviews, researchers observed the reactions of participants as they told their stories and took aligning fieldnotes. Also, observations of the environment/setting, events, and activities occurring in Slidell post Katrina were noted by the researchers.

Data reduction: Codes, categories, and definitions. Merriam (1998) surmises that "making sense out of data involves consolidating, reducing, and interpreting what people have said and what the researcher has seen and read — it is the process of making meaning" (p. 178). Thus, for this study the researchers employed a basic interpretative qualitative approach in order to organize, interpret and make meaning out of the data. Thus, members of the research team read and coded the transcripts of participants independently and then gathered to compare their coding schemes. A collaborative codebook was developed wherein researchers agreed on major categories and themes that cut across the entire data set.

Ensuring quality. To ensure quality and rigor in the research process, a number of approaches were employed in this study. First, multiple investigators and sources of data were triangulated in order to confirm the emerging patterns in the study. Second, transcripts were returned to participants for their review — member checking. And finally, rich, thick descriptions were chosen so that the reader can identify to what extent the findings of our study fit their situations.

RESULTS

Inductive qualitative analysis yielded findings around four major themes: (a) dependence on Godly wisdom; (b) belief in God's promise for provision; (c) reliance on kinship ties; and (d) need for faith-based support. Table 3.2 provides definitions of these major themes.

Dependence on Godly Wisdom

In the midst of a natural disaster, such as Hurricane Katrina, most participants reported the need to seek Godly counsel and guidance for survival. Participants not only prayed on their own, but some received counsel from pastors or religious leaders to leave the area. Jackie described how her pastor, from the pulpit, advised his congregation to leave the area. When she was not considering leaving due to finances, the pastor not only implored the families to leave, but provided the resources to do so. Jackie described this interaction "So we went to church that Sunday morning, our pastor . . . told everybody they needed to leave. And whoever didn't have the finances to go, to see him after service." Participants shared with limited notice that they had to make life and death decisions that affected them and their entire families. In hindsight, Shannon (a 41-year-old-mother) uttered in firm assurance "I just thank God we had the sense to get out of there."

After many years of living and facing life's challenges, Jackie's (a 43-year-old) observation of Katrina was, "But it strengthens your faith in, you know, God!" Hence, individuals' and families' dependence on Godly wisdom was a significant factor in surviving Hurricane Katrina.

Belief in God's Promise for Provision

Experiencing Hurricane Katrina taught survivors in this study many lessons. Often participants spoke of God's divine power and control. When asked how Katrina has impacted her faith, Jackie (a 43-year-old) aptly replied:

> Very strong! You know, I had a lot of faith before this even happened. . . . But it's even made me know that without anything. And that's what I tell people: *You say you want something and you speak it! . . . Life or death is in the power of*

Table 3.2.   Major Themes Revealed by Study Participants

Dependence on Godly Wisdom: Individuals who rely on God for discernment in daily living and practice as well as in unforeseen circumstances.

Belief in God's Promise for Provision: Refers to God's care for humanity. Thus, God blesses supplies, protects, and fulfills promises. And God's faithfulness to His people.

Reliance on Kinship Ties: Refers to the strong dependence on immediate and extended families as well as fictive kin (e.g., church members, neighbors, and friends).

Need for Faith-Based Support: Refers to religious institutions, community based organizations, and non-profits committed to supporting and meeting the needs of Katrina survivors.

God. Whatever you speak, that's what you'll have . . . but if you leave it with me,
you get anything you need. . . . I already . . . you know, had that faith before this!

As evidenced from above, Jackie's survival of Katrina has both reinforced and encouraged her to share her faith.

Echoing Jackie's sentiments, Lynette (a 42-year-old) agreed on the centrality of faith in saying:

> I mean, if it wasn't for [faith], I think a lot of people would've just really lost it! You have to have faith in something. If you don't have faith in God, well, you don't have anything! Because I know I would not be here today had it not been and I know I've been blessed. I have been blessed. I'll tell anybody I've been truly blessed! I may have lost everything I own. The only reason I still have my car is because it was in the airport. So, I lost literally everything I own, but I have been blessed because we didn't lose any family members. And all four days we didn't now if they were dead or alive.

When participants spoke of God's provision and blessings, their focus was not primarily on material goods but also on the value of family. This is best exemplified in Shannon's summation:

> You know, oh my God, count your blessings. Because you know, so many families . . . all their families live in New Orleans . . . all their families live in St. Bernard Parish . . . So they had nowhere to go! No memorabilia left. You know. Everything that their families had owned, treasured, was just gone. You know, count your blessings for just people and families. People were so, so good to us. Oh my gosh!

A few participants stated that they felt guilty for God's provision and blessings. Etta (a 48-year-old), for example, confessed:

> God was truly, truly on my side. That's how I felt. Because I feel like everything comes from Him. So I feel like that He was just truly, truly on my side. I don't know why, because I feel like I am not deserving, you know? But I am still His child. And no matter what . . . no matter . . . what we do, you know. So, I was just truly, truly blessed.

Throughout many dangers and toils, Katrina survivors wholeheartedly affirm their belief in God's promises of provision.

Reliance on Kinship Ties

Many participants in this study reported enduring Hurricane Katrina and its aftermath with the help of their families and fictive kin (i.e., church members, neighbors, and dear friends). Etta for example, in recounting the types of support she received, without hesitation acknowledged first and foremost her family, whom she affectionately describes: "I feel like African-Americans have a strong, strong foundation. I know I had a strong foundation, you know, as a black family." In greater detail, she further recounted the significant role of family following Katrina:

> Well, I was with my family, so I was a little bit fortunate . . . . And I have . . . three nephews and a niece that live [in Houston]. . . . And they just opened their arms, and took us in! And people in their jobs supported them and things that we needed. You know, people took lists of items that we needed. And it was just absolutely phenomenal! So, you know . . . one niece, her husband is a pastor . . . they provided the shelter for [several families from Slidell]. And it was their church congregation and they took in strangers, people that they didn't even know, that they didn't even know, from another area of New Orleans. And they provided them with food, clothing. They wanted to cook for these people. Remember, they had bought all the food and everything. They wanted to prepare the meals for them. But they didn't feel that that was necessary because they had done so much. And they did not charge them anything to stay there. And they were welcome there as long—you know, as long as need be, they were there. As a matter of fact, it was my niece and her other side of the family, her aunt, her cousins. You know, they provided them with beds. Just totally laid them out! And that was a—you know, a true blessing. So I feel ever indebted to [them] . . . because they were just awesome. To take in—you know, somebody that they didn't even know anything about. So, I just feel—out of all of this—I still feel very, very blessed. You know, I just thank God for my life and my family's life.

Etta's reflections exemplify the importance of family and fictive kin overwhelmingly reported by participants in this study.

A few participants elaborated on why and how family and fictive kin became essential when governmental entities failed to protect its citizenry. In recounting how Katrina has affected her faith, Tracey (a 28-year-old Hurricane Katrina survivor who weathered remained in Slidell during the entire storm) boldly declared: "Faith in your family and you keep faith in yourself! But it kind of takes your faith away as far as local government, as far as help-wise." In an impassioned tone, Tony (a 40-year-old) agreed with Tracey by saying:

> . . . the government basically needs to pull themselves together. You know. I mean . . . to say that this is the United States of America—we're supposed to be one of the richest nations, and you know, we can send billions of dollars to other countries to help them; yet, we have a travesty here! . . . On our soil, United States soil! And here it is a year later and we are no closer to pulling our lives together because the government has just not been there. And the people in this area, I mean, basically pulled together [and] took things into their own hands.

And they wanted to come back! You know, we had to come back because we just want a normal life. We want some normalcy back in our lives.

Katrina survivors in the study repeatedly mentioned how they banned together, even independently of governmental support. Thus, kinship ties were essential for the spirituality and basic needs of survivors in this study.

Need for Faith-Based Support

Participants in this study overwhelmingly reported the manifold expressions of generosity by religious institutions, community based, and nonprofit organizations. "Churches have been a blessing all over, and I mean, that's New Orleans to Mississippi you'll hear the same thing. We have these organizations and church groups that came down; and, we've had college groups to come down" recounted Lynette when asked about sources of social support. Participants in this study resoundingly pointed to external sources of support. Ellis (a 63-year-old), for example, referring to religious institutions, non-profits and the Red Cross enthusiastically shared that "They had some church organizations to come down and they gutted five or six houses for me. [They were from] out of town and that was a great help!"

Faith-based support became essential for many participants in this study, as several talked about the lack of support from governmental entities (local and state). Etta painfully explained how she felt:

You know. Living in, as far as I'm concerned, a 4x4—you know, home conditions. You know, with three, four children. I'm just—you know, I'm very, very disappointed in the whole—I guess, like I say, government assistance. You know, just very, very disappointed. What hurt me the most, really, to be honest with you, was to be called a refugee. Because I thought a refugee was somebody from a Third World country, or someone—you know, outside of the United States. And that was just a slap in the face for me. That's how I felt. Because I felt like that— I'm a taxpayer, I'm an American citizen and a taxpayer. And for you to call me a refugee, it's a slap in my face. You know, I work and I contribute to the society. So that was the most hurting thing for me. The entire process, I felt like the entire process of how black Americans, how they were treated, I felt like the entire process was unfair. I didn't feel like they acted—you know, quickly.

Etta was not alone in her experiences. Almost all the participants in this study shared their discontent with the governmental entities as summed up by Vonda (a 61-year-old):

Hey, we're America, here we are treating these people like refugees . . . because I feel like the [federal] government and our own, our local government, should have been able to move a whole lot faster, we have the knowledge and we have the equipment to move . . . people out of harm's way, that bothers me!

By default of all branches of government, it seems, participants expressed that their support during the disaster was from other sources, which led to a dire need of faith-based and other non-governmental support.

DISCUSSION

The purpose of this qualitative study was to explore how religion and spirituality shaped the experiences of African American families living in Slidell, Louisiana in the aftermath of Katrina. This study extends the emerging research literature on the utilization of religious and spiritual practices as a resource that sustained and protected individuals from potentially adverse physical, psychological and financial effects. In this research, the following findings were uncovered: (a) dependence on Godly wisdom; (b) belief in God's promise for provision; (c) reliance on kinship ties; and, (d) need for faith-based support. A discussion of these findings follows as well as implications for families and children surviving natural disasters.

Mattis and Jagers (2001) conceptualize a relational framework to examine religious and spirituality among African Americans. This framework accentuates the significance of an ecological perspective to explore the dynamic relationship individuals experience when fostering and maintaining a connection with God or the Divine. The results of the present study begin to substantiate this framework. At the individual level, the participants articulated that religion and spirituality minifies the impact of negative emotional consequences of Katrina. To illustrate, reliance on faith (i.e., God) helped individuals cope and understand the magnitude of the loss of life, material possessions, and property. Additionally, participants expressed sincere gratitude regarding the safety of family members and retention of personal belongings. The overwhelming magnitude of Katrina enabled participants to reflect in awe on God's creation and simultaneously express gratitude for God's goodness and mercy.

Living through the aftermath of the storm, participants described culturally specific coping strategies that undergird aspects of the relational framework at the family level. Participation in religious and spiritual activities potentially creates and deepens interactions among individuals that sustain different types of personal relationships. The relational model at this level emphasizes the diverse religious socialization process and spiritual rituals African Americans engage in to cope with positive and negative life circumstances. Mattis and Jagers (2001) describe the family relational framework as incorporating collective and spiritual cultural-specific group centered coping approaches to seek out significant others like family, extended family, elders and fictive kin networks in providing instrumental support such as clothing, financial assistance, food, and shelter. Collective coping "is conceptualized as an African American cultural value and practice that places the group interests above that of an individual. In this coping style African Americans rely on group centered activities for managing stressful situations" (Utsey, Bolden, Williams, Lee, Lanier et al., 2007, pp. 124–125). Likewise, the previous authors continue to explain how spiritual coping promotes resiliency and provides African Americans an opportunity to comprehend the universe and their relationship with a higher power (Utsey, Adams, & Bolden, 2003). Both of these coping strategies illustrate the self-help tradition (for more details, see Lincoln & Mamiya, 1990 and Thomas, 1992) among African Americans to assist not only family members but also utilize fictive kinship networks to meet financial and psychological needs. Thus, the results from this study corroborate the relational framework wherein family relationships help in facilitating the religious and spiritual life among African American hurricane survivors.

Historically, the Black church has always functioned in the primary role of spreading the Gospel to congregation members, and has operated in many different roles providing leadership to develop the community in areas of education, politics, plus economics. At the community level, the involvement in "church work" such as feeding the poor, caring for the elderly, ministering to the least of these, and visiting the sick and shut-in, by most African American faith communities facilitate intimacy, interdependence and reliance on congregation members and others that encourages a sense of community and social obligations to the broader society (Mattis & Jagers, 2001). Although the mainstream media and some empirical research have questioned the utility of the Black church, Katrina survivors in this study emphasized the importance of the informal support networks among faith communities sustained them through the disaster. In many cases, the participants elucidated that the initial care received to assist them came from African American church members and clergy. Responding to the clarion call for social justice to prevail, the church and kinship networks clearly compensated for the absence of immediate interventions by local, state, and federal governments.

IMPLICATIONS

Katrina and its aftermath exposed the underbelly of race, poverty, and class in American society. As a result, a national dialogue must examine these intersections and seek solutions. Therefore, the media should serve as a catalyst and cultural critic for the dialogue of race, class, and poverty as well as confront its own biases in how it perpetuates negative stereotypes of the poor and people of color. The future of families relies on how we as a society redress these injustices.

How could African American families and children be better prepared for life's unknowns and ambiguities, such as natural disasters? This study illustrates that though it is impossible to prepare for every potential life event, it is essential that families and children cling to and cultivate their core cultural, religious, and spiritual rootedness. Hence, African American families must continue to nurture strong family support and social networks to ensure physical and emotional survival.

The findings of this study strongly indicate that faith-based, community, and other non-profit organizations, tend to serve as the central means of support to families and children when disasters occur. Thus, just as health and safety entities prepare disaster and emergency response plans, clergy, educators, counselors, and social workers should do so as well. What this study brings to light is that the outreach and care-giving professions must not only attend to the physical and emotional needs of families and children, but the religious and spiritual as well, during natural disasters.

Limitations of the Study

While the study provides rich information regarding the impact of faith, additional research is needed to address other aspects of the experiences for Katrina survivors (e.g. housing, insurance, and governmental assistance). First, the sample size is relatively small compared to the number of African Americans who were adversely affected in the storm. Second, the sample only included African Americans in one city of the Gulf Coast Region. Finally, the majority of the sample was female. The strength of this study was the importance of understanding how these African American families utilized coping mechanisms through their religion and spiritual grounding to whether them through the storm.

CONCLUSION

Hurricane Katrina was a devastating storm that changed millions of people living in the Gulf Cost region. One thing is clear for Hurricane survivors who participated in this study—faith and spirituality played a significant role in sustaining these African American families. Moreover, as a community and society, we cannot discount the spiritual and emotional impact of natural disasters on children. They are often the unforeseen victims wherein their spiritual distress doesn't always manifest. We hope this study adds to the growing body of knowledge related to religion and spirituality, which is the bedrock of many African American communities. As we shared participants' voices of faith, hope, and love for their families, it is clear—no matter a tornado, hurricane or storm—with God, these survivors will remain steadfast in protecting their families.

REFERENCES

Bogdan, R., & Biklen, S. K. (2003). *Qualitative research for education: An introduction to theory and methods* (4th ed.). Boston: Allyn and Bacon.

Bowen-Reid, T. L. & Smalls, C. (2004). Stress, spirituality and health promoting behaviors among African American college students. *Western Journal of Black Studies, 28*, (1), 283–291.

Briggs, X. (2006). After Katrina: Rebuilding lives and places. *City and Community,* 5(2), 119–128.

Ellison, C.G. (1991). Religious involvement and the subjective quality of family life. *Journal of Health and Social Behavior, 32*, 80–89.

Ellison, C. G. (1998). Religion, health, and well-being among African Americans. *African American Research Perspectives, 4*, 94–103.

Ellison, C.G., & Gay, D.A. (1990). Region, religious commitment, and life satisfaction among black Americans. *Sociological Quarterly, 31*, 123–147.

Koenig, H. G., McCullough, M. E. & Larson, D. B. (2001). *Handbook of religion and health.* New York: Oxford University Press.

Kyeremateng, K. N. (1998). *Global religious viewpoints.* Accra: Ghana; Sebewie Publishers.

Lawson, & Thomas (2007). Wading in the Waters: Spirituality and older Black Katrina survivors. *Journal of Health Care for the Poor and Underserved,* 18, 341–354.

Lincoln, E. C., & Mamiya, L. H. (1990). *The Black church in the African American experience.* Durham, NC: Duke University Press.

Louisiana Speaks. Long-term community recovery planning (2006). *St. Tammany Parish Disaster Needs Assessment.* Retrieved, July 21, 2007, from http: //www .louisiana speaks-parishplans.org/IndParishHomepage_BaselineNeedsAssessment. cfm?EntID=16

Mattis, J. S. (1997). The spiritual well-being of African Americans: A preliminary analysis. *Journal of Prevention and Intervention in the Community, 16*, 103–120.

Mattis, J. S. (2000). African American women's definitions of spirituality and religiosity. *Journal of Black Psychology, 26*, 101–122.

Mattis, J. S., & Jagers, R. J. (2001). A relational framework for the study of religiosity and spirituality in the lives of African Americans. *Journal of Community Psychology, 29* (5), 519–539.

Mattis, J. S., Fontenot, D. L. & Hatcher-Kay, C. A. (2003). Religiosity, racism, and dispositional optimism among African Americans. *Personality and Individual Differences, 34* (6), 1025–1038.

McNulty, K., Livneh, H., & Wilson, L. M. (2004). Perceived uncertainty, spiritual well-being, and psychosocial adaptation in individuals with multiple sclerosis. *Rehabilitation Psychology, 49*, 91–99.

Merriam, S. B. (1998). *Qualitative research and case study applications in education* (2nd ed.). San Francisco: Jossey-Bass.

Paragament K., & Maton K. (2000). Religion in American life: A community psychology perspective. In J. Rappaport & E. Seidman (Eds.), *Handbook in Community Psychology* (pp. 495–522). New York : Kluwer Academic/Plenum.

Patton, M. Q. (2002). *Qualitative research and evaluation methods* (3rd ed.). Thousand Oaks, CA: Sage.

Rivera, J. D., & Miller, D.S. (March, 2007). Continually Neglected: Situating natural disasters in the African American experience. *Journal of Black Studies*, 37 (4), 502–522.

Sanders, S., Bowie, S.L., & Bowie, Y.D. (2003). Lesson learned on forced relocation of older adults: The impact of Hurricane Andrew on health, mental health and social support on public housing residents. *Journal of Gerontological Social Work,* 40 *(4)*, 23–35.

Sharkey, P. (March, 2007). Survival and Death in New Orleans: An Empirical look at the human impact of Katrina. *Journal of Black Studies*, 37 (4), 482–501.

Taylor, R., Chatters, L. & Levin, J. (2004). *Religion in the Lives of African Americans: Social, Psychological, and Health Perspectives.* Newbury Park, CA: Sage Publications.

Thomas, R. (1992). *Life is what we make it: building Black community in Detroit, 1915–1945.* Bloomington: Indiana University Press.

Utsey, S. O., Adams, E. P., & Bolden, M. (2000). Development and validation of the Africultural Coping Systems Inventory. *Journal of Black Psychology, 26*, 194–215.

Utsey, S. O., Bolden, M. A., Williams, O., Lee, A., Lanier Y., & Newsome. C. (2007). Spiritual Well-Being as a Mediator of the Relation between Culture-Specific Coping and Quality of Life in a Community Sample of African Americans. *Journal of Cross-Cultural Psychology, 38* (2), 123–136.

Zakour, M. J., & Harrell, E. B. (2003). Access to disaster services: Social work interventions for vulnerable populations. *Journal of Social Service Research, 30* (2), 27–54.

Chapter Four

Culturally Responsive Literacy in the Aftermath of Katrina

Yolanda L. Dunston

ABSTRACT

The young children who experienced Hurricane Katrina have memories of this horrific event, and many are still living in conditions that form a constant reminder of the disaster that they survived. Because they were small children when Katrina occurred, some of their memories may be chaotic, frightening, and confusing. They may have even developed some misconceptions about weather, their personal safety, and their ability to lead normal lives. Several books have been published to help children understand and cope with real weather disasters (e.g., Jackson, 2005; Mercier, 2006; Miller, 2006; Wallner, 2006). Some have specifically been written in response to Hurricane Katrina, often as a collaboration between young children and the teacher/guides with whom they actually experienced the event (Mann's Miracles, 2006; McGrath, 2006; Visser, 2006). These books provide factual information as well as personal accounts on the subject of weather disasters, including how families can prepare for a hurricane, the various ways communities can be affected by hurricanes, and how communities can begin to rebuild after a hurricane. Effective use of these books can help young children to grow socially, emotionally, and academically. This section presents a variety of literacy activities to be used as part of an integrated thematic unit appropriate for children in the primary grades, based on a text set of books related to hurricanes.

HEALING THROUGH LITERACY

In order for learning to take place, new information must be integrated with what the learner already knows (Rumelhart, 1980). In the area of literacy,

63

reading comprehension is enhanced when students have prior knowledge about a topic, and are able to make personal connections as they read and listen to text. When children hear and read stories about hurricanes, they realize that other children have experienced similar disasters. Consequently, they may be more able to accept their feelings and move forward towards a sense of normalcy.

A thematic unit on Hurricanes would serve multiple purposes. First, it would incorporate a variety of informational texts, which would help the children understand the science behind hurricanes and other weather disasters. This scientific awareness can promote preparedness for such disasters in the future, and can help children learn ways to cope with those disasters, should they occur. However, because general weather-related science concepts are typically part of the elementary school science curriculum, they are not the focus of this unit described here. Rather, the suggested activities focus on the children's authentic experiences.

When planned appropriately, a thematic unit can provide a safe context for children to express their feelings about the disaster they recently experienced. The following activities incorporates each of the six language arts: reading, writing, listening, speaking, viewing, and visually representing. However, at the heart of this unit are the expressive areas of language, which are speaking (e.g., informal discussion and dramatization), visually representing (e.g., drawing), and writing (e.g., personal accounts) because engaging in these activities helps to defuse feelings and to make sense of experiences following traumatic events (FEMA, 2007). According to FEMA, defusing is

> *"[a] supportive, personalized, safe, interactive process between individuals in small groups with facilitator(s) that provides/facilitates clarity and complete expression of the event/experiences. It can be emotional. It can help children to develop coping skills and to heal"* (p. 3).

By providing opportunities for drawing, talking, and writing about a disaster such as Hurricane Katrina, young children can begin to understand that

- their experiences are shared by others;
- their thoughts, fears, and concerns about the experiences are shared by others; and
- they can heal and gradually begin to lead normal lives.

Finally, by getting involved in group activities (e.g., fundraising, pen pals, story publishing, etc.), the children can develop a sense of connectedness and decrease feelings of powerlessness. Essentially, by engaging in talk and drawing activities in the following thematic unit, children can begin to understand, cope, and move forward after a natural disaster.

INTEGRATED LITERACY ACTIVITIES FOR THE
PRIMARY GRADES: HURRICANES AND WEATHER SAFETY

National Standards and Indicators Addressed

Science Standards for Elementary School Teachers

Standard 3: Elementary teachers have a broad knowledge and understanding of the major concepts in science.

Indicator 3: Teachers have knowledge of basic earth science concepts including:

- Planetary astronomy (objects in the sky, changes in the earth and sky, and weather)
- Properties of earth materials (rocks, minerals, fossils, water, air)
- Earth dynamics and systems
- Interaction of earth and living systems including management of natural resources and pollution.

English Language Arts and Literacy Standards for Elementary School Teachers

Standard 1: Elementary teachers have a broad knowledge and understanding of the major concepts in English Language Arts and Literacy.

Indicator 4: Teachers understand the elementary school child's social, cultural, linguistic, cognitive, and affective backgrounds as they relate to the ability to develop effective communication processes (listening, speaking, reading, and writing).

Indicator 5: Teachers know and understand that reading is taught as a process of constructing meaning through the interaction of the reader's existing knowledge, the information suggested by the written language, and the context of the reading situation.

Indicator 6: Teachers understand the importance of literacy for personal and social growth.

SUGGESTED LITERACY AND LANGUAGE ARTS ACTIVITIES

The following section presents literacy/language arts activities to be used within a larger thematic unit for young children (kindergarten—third grade) who have experienced a hurricane or other weather disaster. Each activity begins with a description of the general procedure, and is followed by suggestions for tailoring the procedure to meet the specific needs of the children. Finally, the language arts skills and strategies addressed in the procedure are listed.

Table 4.1.   Language Arts Strategies and Skills (Tompkins, 2006)

Strategies

Activating background knowledge* (B)	Noticing non-verbal cues
Blending, segmenting	Organizing
Brainstorming	Playing with words, language
Connecting* (D)	Predicting* (B)
Determining viewpoint	Proofreading
Drawing conclusions	Questioning* (B, D)
Evaluating	Revising
Identifying big ideas* (D)	Setting purposes
Making inferences* (D)	Summarizing* (D, A)
Monitoring	Visualizing* (D)

Skills

Comprehension Skills—*fact vs. opinion, compare/contrast, recognizing genres and structures** (D)

Print Skills—*sounding out words, noticing word families, using root words and affixes to decode and spell, using abbreviations** (D, A)

Study Skills—*skimming/scanning, taking notes, making clusters, previewing a book prior to reading** (B, D, A)

Language Skills—*identifying word meanings, noticing idioms, dividing words into syllables, choosing synonyms** (B, D, A)

Reference Skills—*alphabetizing, using a dictionary, reading and making graphs and diagrams** (A)

Note: The * indicates comprehension skills and strategies for use with informational text. The letter(s) in parentheses indicates the reading phase when the strategies are most effective (Before, During, or After reading). From Kletzien and Dreher (2004), *Informational Text in K-3 Classrooms: Helping Children Read and Write.*

Activity: Journal Writing

General Procedure: Provide blank journals for all students. Tell students that these are personal journals in which they can write about anything they wish. Time should be set aside each day in class for journal writing. Students should write something each day. Younger students may also choose to draw pictures. The print may be their own invented spelling or dictation printed by a teacher. Entries are not graded, but the teacher must check to see that something has been written or drawn each day. Provide a secure place where students can place their journals if there is something that they would like read by the teacher. Otherwise, students should feel confident that their work in these journals is personal and will not be read or shared with others.

Thematic Connection: Journal writing provides an excellent opportunity for students to express some of their personal thoughts about Hurricane Katrina, without concerns of having to share those thoughts publicly.

Language Arts Strategies: brainstorming, evaluating, playing with words/language

Language Arts Skills: print, language

Table 4.2.   Content Area Word Wall

The list below is extensive, but by no means exhaustive. Teachers should select words for study that are relevant to the students in the classroom and appropriate for the activities presented. Students may choose to use the words when writing, and should be encouraged to spell them correctly, depending on the assignment purpose.

abandoned	donations	Katrina	relief
aftermath	electricity	landfall	relocate
assistance	emergency	levee	repair
batteries	evacuate	lightning	rescue
category	FEMA	mayor	restore
center	flashlight	MREs	safety
coast	flood	neighborhood	search
community	forecaster	ocean	season
damage	Gulf Coast	plan	spinning
debris	help	prepare	storm
destroy	hurricane	rebuild	supplies
disaster	inland	recover	

Activity: Double Entry Journals

General Procedure: This activity follows a teacher read aloud or students' independent reading of a selected text. Provide blank journals for each student, or even a single sheet of plain paper. Students draw a line down the middle of the page. Label the two columns "Quote" and "Response." On the left side of the line, students write a quote from the text which has personal meaning. On the right side of the line, students write why the quote stands out to them.

Thematic Connection: This is a wonderful extension activity to follow reading some of the books written by children who experienced Hurricane Katrina (e.g., McGrath, 2006; Mercier, 2006). For example, after hearing The Storm (McGrath, 2006) read aloud, students would select meaningful quotes from the book and follow-up with personal responses related to their own hurricane experiences.

Language Arts Strategies: activating background knowledge, connecting, inferencing, evaluating

Language Arts Skills: comprehension, language, reference

Activity: Young Children's Letters

General Procedure: In this activity, children write letters to authors of books they are reading. While writing, they make connections between the authors and themselves, and ask questions of the authors in an attempt to understand how or why the books were written, or to simply learn more about the author.

Thematic Connection: Children can write letters to authors of the hurricane-related books. Some of the authors are children, making this an excellent opportunity for children to connect with other children who experienced similar disasters in a pen pal environment. Children may also write letters to public officials regarding hurricane preparedness or efforts to rebuild in their communities.

Language Arts Strategies: brainstorming, connecting, setting purposes, questioning, evaluating, proofreading, revising

Language Arts Skills: comprehension

Activity: Personal Narratives

General Procedure: When composing personal narratives, students write personal stories from their own perspective. The narratives follow a basic story structure, including a beginning, a middle, and an end. Prior to writing, children may be encouraged to brainstorm through drawing.

Thematic Connection: Students write about Hurricane Katrina from their own perspectives. In some cases, the personalized account may not follow the conventional story structure; rather, it may be a fragment of a larger, more complex story. For example, the story may reveal the part of the hurricane experience that is most prominent in the child's memory, or the one that is least difficult to express. Additionally, one child may write a single sentence about the frightening sounds of the hurricane, while another child may write several paragraphs that move through the sequence of planning, evacuation, searching for pets, and rebuilding.

Note: Students' personal narratives can also be edited, revised, and compiled in a book that can be used for classroom reading, or published commercially for a broader audience. As with some of the books in the text set written by children and published commercially, the publishers may donate a percentage of the profits to aid communities in rebuilding after a disaster.

Language Arts Strategies: activating background knowledge, brainstorming, determining viewpoint, setting purposes, evaluating, identifying big ideas, making inferences, organizing, playing with words/language, proofreading, revising, summarizing

Language Arts Skills: comprehension skills (fact vs. opinion, recognizing genres/structures), print skills (sounding out words), language skills (choosing synonyms)

Activity: Found Poems

General Procedure: Students collect words and phrases from texts they are reading, then arrange the collection into lines to create a free-form poem.

Thematic Connection: Texts can include informational books about hurricanes, true storybooks about hurricanes, and newspapers and magazine articles related to Hurricane Katrina. The following poem below was written using only phrases found in Hurricane! (London, 1998):

The sky fell
The wind ripped
Rain so solid, it was like driving underwater
The wind died down
The rain stopped hammering
All was silent
Everything around us had changed.

Language Arts Strategies: organizing, setting purposes, playing with words/language, proofreading, revising, summarizing, visualizing
Language Arts Skills: comprehension, study skills, language skills

Activity: Story Retelling

General Procedure: After hearing stories read aloud, or reading stories independently, students can summarize the stories by providing the main events in order.

Thematic Connection: Some of the stories from the text set are written in simple story structure, and are more suitable for retelling, for example, Sergio and the Hurricane (Wallner, 2000) and Hurricane! (London, 1998). It may be helpful to have students illustrate their story parts before retelling, perhaps in a 3-column format (beginning, middle, ending), or with pictures that represent the main events in sequence.

Language Arts Strategies: organizing, identifying big ideas
Language Arts Skills: comprehension, language

Activity: Dramatizing

General Procedure: Students are provided an opportunity to act out stories or experiences. Performances may be scripted or unscripted, rehearsed or improvised. Students may choose to use puppets, props, costumes, or sets, but these are not required. The audience may be the current class, or an outside audience such as another class or a group of parents.

Thematic Connection: As with story retelling, some books are written in a structure that lend easily to dramatizations. Additionally, students may dramatize actual events that occurred during the time of Hurricane Katrina. Finally, students might choose to role play responses to disasters, which may help them to think clearly and act quickly, should another disaster occur.

Language Arts Strategies: brainstorming, identifying big ideas, determining viewpoint, making inferences

Language Arts Skills: comprehension, language

Activity: Show and Tell—Sharing Personal Experiences

General Procedure: Children verbally share stories of their own personal experiences. Props may be used to enhance audience engagement.

Thematic Connection: Children may talk about their own family's experience during the hurricane. They may bring props such as stuffed animals, photos or hand-drawn illustrations of their home or bedroom, or other special items that support the story.

Language Arts Strategies: identifying big ideas, organizing, playing with words/language, *summarizing.*

Language Arts Skills: *comprehension, language*

Activity: Show and Tell—Me Boxes and Disaster Kits

General Procedure: When creating "Me Boxes," children collect items that are of personal significance. "Me Boxes" are often covered with colored paper and decorated with pictures or stickers selected by the child. The contents of the box are shown and explained to the group.

Thematic Connection: Students can prepare "Me Boxes" or "Disaster Kits" for sharing with classmates. For "Me Boxes," students can collect several items that hold personal significance, which they might want to have ready in case of a disaster. For example, students might fill the box with a favorite book, stuffed animal or small toy, family photo, CD of favorite music, or other special mementos that they would like to have with them in case the family needs to leave the home in a hurry. For "Disaster Kits," students collect items their family would need in case of an emergency—including batteries, water bottles, important documents, and a small first aid kit. These construction projects offer an opportunity for children and parents to work together and to discuss important matters related to hurricane and disaster preparedness.

Language Arts Strategies: brainstorming, evaluating, identifying big ideas, organizing

Language Arts Skills: Comprehension, language.

CHILDREN'S LITERATURE DATABASE

As a final supplement to the suggested activities, a database has been created based on a set of children's books related to hurricanes. The books come from a wide range of genres, such as narrative informational (non-fiction content in a narrative format) to historical accounts (also presented in narrative format), and non-fictional storybooks (personal accounts told in narrative format from children's perspectives). Some tradition fiction books are included as well. For each book, publishing information is provided, as well information regarding intended age groups, book description, and further ideas for classroom instruction. (See Database.)

FINAL THOUGHTS

When used carefully, the expressive activities suggested above can provide a safe environment for children to learn about natural disasters, to express and sort out their feelings about disasters they have experienced, and to make social and emotional progress after those disasters. Moreover, the unit's literacy activities can promote preparedness for such disasters in the future, and can help children learn ways to cope with those disasters, should they occur.

Table 4.3. Data Base

Author	Title Publisher, ©	Audience	GENRE/Overview	Ideas for Instruction
Cole, Joanna	The Magic School Bus Inside a Hurricane Scholastic, 1995	Grades 2–4 Portions can be read aloud to Kindergarten and 1st grade students	NARRATIVE INFORMATIONAL Mrs. Frizzle's class boards the magic school bus on an educational adventure inside a hurricane. Story provides factual information related to atmosphere, clouds, weather, hurricanes. Scientific facts presented in story form, with cartoon illustrations. *Can be used with accompanying guide featuring hands-on science and pre/post-reading activities (G. Young, Teacher Created Resources, © 1996).*	Listening for important information Note taking Fact vs. Fiction (Real vs. Fantasy)
London, Jonathan	Hurricane! Harper Collins, 1998	Read Aloud, grades K–3	HISTORICAL ACCOUNT The author retells the story of his experience surviving a hurricane as a young boy in Puerto Rico. The story progresses from preparation, to clean-up, to resuming normal lives again.	Listening for similarities, connections Visualization Publishing as a means of healing
Mann's Miracles	When the Hurricane Blew: Clear Horizon, 2006	Read Aloud, grades K–3	HISTORICAL STORYBOOK, EDUCATIONAL ACTIVITY BOOK Subtitle: "A Story, Tips, and Games, Created by Hurricane Kids for Hurricane Kids." The book was written and illustrated by 4th graders from Gulf Breeze, Florida, who experienced Hurricane Ivan on September 16, 2004. The story is one continuous account, and is followed by tips for before/after a hurricane and child-created games to play while being evacuated or displaced.	Listening for similarities, connections Voice, word choice in writing Visualization Publishing as a means of healing

Author	Title	Reading Level	Description	Skills
McGrath, Barbara Barbieri	The Storm: Students of Biloxi, Mississippi, Remember Hurricane Katrina Charlesbridge, 2006	Read Aloud, grades K–3	NON-FICTIONAL STORYBOOK The story, which weaves children's illustrations and personal accounts following Hurricane Katrina, begins with the evacuation and ends with families' efforts to rebuild and regain normal lives.	Combining resources to tell a story Listening for similarities, connections Voice, word choice in writing Visualization Publishing as a means of healing
Mercier, Deirdre McLauglin	Yesterday We Had a Hurricane Bumblebee Publishing, 2006	Read Aloud, K–1 Independent Reading, Grades 1–3	NON-FICTIONAL STORYBOOK This book was written by a teacher/counselor after experiencing Hurricane Charley in 2004. Written specifically for her preschool students, the author presents the story as seen through the eyes of a young child.	Basic understanding of hurricanes Listening for similarities, connections Publishing as a means of healing
Miller, Mara	Hurricane Katrina Strikes the Gulf Coast: Disaster and Survival Enslow Publishers, 2006	Intended for Intermediate Grades; Portions can be read aloud to younger students	EXPOSITORY INFORMATIONAL True story of one of the worst disasters in American history. Survivor stories. Actual photos. Includes glossary and resources (print, internet) for additional reading.	Listening Comprehension Summarizing Understanding Text Structures Using quotes Sequencing Events
Pitt, Steve	Rain Tonight: A Story of Hurricane Hazel Tundra Books, 2004	Read aloud, grades 3–5	HISTORICAL ACCOUNT A young girl tells the story of Hurricane Hazel, which occurred in 1954. Personal journals, newspaper articles, and personal interviews are used to make the story authentic. Includes additional factual information about hurricanes in page margins; black and white illustrations, and a section with real photos depicting the hurricane's devastation.	Combining resources to tell a story Listening for similarities, connections

(continued)

Table 4.3. *(continued)*

Author	Title Publisher, ©	Audience	GENRE/Overview	Ideas for Instruction
MSimon, Seymour	Hurricanes Harper Collins, 2003	Grades 2-4 Portions can be read aloud to Kindergarten and 1st grade students	NON-FICTION Full-color, full-page photographs combined with well-structured text provide basic information about hurricanes, as well as specific accounts of hurricanes devastating the Caribbean Islands and the United States.	Understanding text structures Listening for important information Note taking Summarizing
Visser, Reona	Story of a Storm: A book about Hurricane Katrina Quail Ridge Press, 2006	Read aloud, Kindergarten; Independent Reading, Grades 1–3	HISTORICAL STORYBOOK Simple yet powerful sentences and elaborate collages tell the story of Hurricane Katrina through the eyes of some of its youngest victims. Thirty children, grades K–8, worked on the book with the guidance of a local teacher, while their parents searched the debris for belongings. Long Beach, Mississippi.	Listening for similarities, connections Voice, word choice in writing Visualization Publishing as a means of healing
Wallner, Alexandra	Sergio and the Hurricane Henry Holt & Co., 2000	Read aloud, Grades K–3	FICTION Picture book depicting the story of a young boy whose family endures a hurricane in San Juan, Puerto Rico. Sergio learns how hurricanes affect people and communities	Comparison—text to experiences How To Stories (How to prepare for a hurricane) Generating Lists

Chapter Five

Success Lessons: Select Public Schools Weather the Storm

Alisa Taliaferro, Laura Onafowora, and Helen Jones

INTRODUCTION

Hurricane Katrina struck some of the poorest and most vulnerable communities in the United States. Median incomes in New Orleans and the other affected areas are significantly below the national average. The poverty rate in New Orleans prior to the storm was 23 percent, 76 percent higher than the national average of 13.1 percent. In Louisiana, African Americans comprise 31.5 percent of the population, but 69 percent of the children are in poverty (U.S. Census Bureau, 2004 adjusted).

The storm at the end of August in 2005 made a bad situation even worse. New Orleans victims of Katrina predominantly were African Americans living in poor neighborhoods with high unemployment and low levels of education. The lives of these people were devastated further by the disaster. According to the U.S. Department of Education, Katrina displaced 372,000 students. Approximately 700 schools were damaged or destroyed. Government assistance is needed to replace student and personnel data, school district information systems, instructional materials and equipment, and other education resources.

As one looks to the future of any area that fits the characteristics of concentrated poverty, glimpses of hope always center on education. In his autobiography, *Mirror to America* (2005), John Hope Franklin asserts that the pursuit of knowledge came to be one of the great preoccupations of African Americans and education was viewed by many as the single greatest opportunity to escape proscriptions and indignities.

UNEXPECTED OUTCOMES

Drs. Jones and Taliaferro spent the week of June 4, 2006, in New Orleans, nine months after the hurricane. While in New Orleans we visited schools and toured the city. As expected, we found that teachers, administrators, staff, students, and parents are facing numerous challenges with the reopening of schools.

First, enrollment is an issue because so many families have not returned to New Orleans and there is uncertainty about how many families will actually come back home. According to a 2005 U.S. Census Report, there were 492,912 households in New Orleans pre-Katrina and 285,106 post-Katrina. Some teachers and other staff have not returned. All four of the schools have open enrollment, although they did not before Katrina.

Second, the student data system is almost nonexistent at some schools. Very little student information is available. Without records, it is hard even to determine grade placement.

Third, with change come unfulfilled expectations and communication problems that frustrate both students and parents.

In spite of the challenges, we were impressed with the warmth of teachers, administrators, and staff. There was a sense that "we're in this together."

We had not expected to hear so many stories of pain and suffering. School personnel, taxicab drivers, hotel workers, and others we encountered wanted to tell their stories. They were powerful stories. Imagine coming home to find everything in the refrigerator spoiled, the furniture destroyed, baby pictures gone, the car flooded and undrivable, and the mildew and odors unbearable. "Everything I accumulated in fifty-five years is gone," said one woman. A taxicab driver who also drove a school bus said that he had learned from a co-worker that all of the school bus drivers had been fired. No one had been willing to tell the drivers in person, and no reason had been given. In addition, the people we met talked about friends and co-workers they had not seen or heard about. They wonder if their friends are dead or alive.

Touring the lower ninth ward brought tears to our eyes. Houses were gutted, debris clogged the streets, trees remained atop buildings, and abandoned cars were everywhere. It was hard to believe what we were seeing remained a year after the hurricane. So much of it brought personal reflection and questions. Did the levees have to breech? Why did the poor bear the weight of this disaster? There are so many unanswered questions. At the same time there was a sense of being witnesses to history, given the time to listen to stories and show compassion in a truly unparalleled American experience. We were left with the renewed convictions that our chosen profession is as important as it has ever been, and that the work for equity and social justice is timeless.

BACKGROUND: EDUCATION PRE-KATRINA

One school district serves all of New Orleans, the New Orleans Public Schools (NOPS), also known as the Orleans Parish School Board. When schools opened on August 18, 2005, 124 Orleans Parish public schools served 56,000 students (New Orleans Public School System). During the 2004–2005 school year, over 95 percent of those students were of ethnic or racial minorities in the U.S. Blacks comprised the largest portion of the minority students. Over 75 percent of all students met income guidelines to receive free or reduced-price lunches (Hill and Hannaway, 2006, 4). As is common in urban districts, some Orleans Parish public schools were among the worst in the country. In *Come Hell or High Water*, Michael Dyson states that New Orleans has a 40 percent illiteracy rate; over 50 percent of African-American ninth graders won't graduate in four years. Louisiana expends an average of $4,724 per student and has the third-lowest rank for teacher salaries in the nation." (Dyson, 2006, 8) Between African American and Caucasian students, an achievement gap of 50.6 points existed in English and a 52.8 point gap in math. The achievement gap between African-American and Caucasian students in New Orleans was twice as high as that for all of Louisiana. Also, in 2004–2005, 63 percent of schools in the New Orleans Public School System were deemed academically unacceptable, whereas only 8 percent of schools across Louisiana were academically unacceptable ("Recovery Plan," 2006, 8).

In 2003 the Louisiana State Legislature passed a law calling for the takeover of schools that deemed to have "failed" under the school and district accountability program. A failed school was defined as one that had been identified as "academically unacceptable" for four years or longer. The law allows for the operation of a special state Recovery School District (RSD), to be administered by the Louisiana Department of Education and subject to the authority of the Louisiana Board of Elementary and Secondary Education (Recovery Plan, 2006, 12). Under this legislation, the state declared the Orleans Parish School District to be in academic crisis in 2004 and seized control of five schools, re-opening them as charters (Hill, and Hannaway, 2006, 3).

In July 2005 the school district was facing a $25 to $30 million deficit for 2005–2006. At the behest of the Louisiana Department of Education, the Orleans Parish School District entered into a contract with Alvarez and Marsal, LLC, a nationally recognized turn-around firm to manage the finances and central office functions of the system (Hill and Hannaway, 2006, 2). Their work was just beginning prior to Katrina.

It's pretty clear that the hurricane and flooding from the levee breeches just made a bad situation even worse.

BACKGROUND: EDUCATION POST-KATRINA

The hurricane and flooding destroyed most of the public education system. Teachers, students, administrators, school board members, bus drives and others were forced to evacuate. They ended up in nearby Baton Rouge, Mississippi, Texas, Florida and other states. Eighty-four schools were flooded, and others had severe wind and/or mold damage. Also, the school administration building was damaged to the extent that it could no longer be used. The New Orleans parochial school system, which educated 40 percent of New Orleans' students, was also devastated (Hill and Hann-away, 2006, 1).

On December 30, 2005, President Bush signed the Hurricane Education Recovery Act (HERA) into law. According to the U.S. Department of Education, over $1.6 billion in funds from HERA were made available to reopen schools in the Gulf Coast region and to help educate students across the country displaced or affected by Hurricanes Katrina and Rita. More than 1,100 schools—public, private and parochial—remained closed two weeks following the storms. Public and private school enrollment in New Orleans stands at about 30 percent of the pre-Katrina level.

New Orleans has a variety of different types of public schools; those run by the local school board, those run by the state, and those run by charter groups. In November 2005, the Louisiana Legislature expanded the definition of a failed school. The state now included schools in which students scored below the state average and systems that had been declared to be in "academic crisis" because at least one system school was labeled as failing for four or more years (Recovery Plan, 2006, 12). As a result of this legislation, 107 of Orleans Parish's struggling public schools were transferred to the authority of the RSD. In the state take over of most New Orleans public schools, 7, 500 employees (including 4,000 teachers) were dismissed ("Democracy Now Report," June 20, 2006, 2). This situation proved to be a nightmare for so many people who were already traumatized by the hurricane and flooding. They didn't know how they would make ends meet, and that's putting it mildly.

The president of the New Orleans school board said it would be at least a year before any schools could reopen. But schools did slowly begin to reopen. Near the end of November 2005, Ben Franklin Elementary School was the first public school to reopen. It took a lot of hard work and political pressure from politicians, parents, administrators, teachers, and students to get the schools reopened. Later, McMain Secondary and McDonogh 35 High School reopened, followed by New Orleans Math and Science magnet school and Bethune Elementary on the east bank. By the end of December, there were about two thousand students enrolled in six public schools in Orleans. Many of the students traveled many miles to attend school. Unfortunately, some students ended up being out of school for a year.

Still, as of October 20, 2006, fewer than half the city's public schools had reopened. Five schools are being operated by the Orleans Parish school board, charter groups run thirty-one of the schools, and seventeen are run by the state. Total enrollment is about twenty-five thousand students, less than half of what it was pre-Katrina (Louisiana Department of Education).

Various initiatives are underway to try to improve public schools in New Orleans. The U.S. Department of Education provided over $20 million through a special charter school grant to Louisiana to help open or reopen charter schools in hurricane-effected areas. This enabled public schools in New Orleans to reopen as charter schools. The grant left many officials, educators, and parents angry that they felt the pressure to open traditional public schools as charter schools. Supporters of charters promote them as a way to offer parents choice and strengthen the education system. Critics argue that they will erode the public schools tradition. The debate goes on in New Orleans. Mayor Ray Nagin led an initiative to improve education through his "Bring New Orleans Back" (BNOB) Commission in January 2006. The commission's Education Committee has provided a blueprint for restoring and transforming schools. The final report has thirty-three major recommendations, based on practices modeled from across the country. Emphases are placed on concentrating as much authority as possible at the local schools level, holding principals and teachers more accountable for school performance, clustering similar schools into networks of eight to ten to better share ideas, and lowering teacher/student ratios. The goal is for New Orleans public school students to average standardized test scores in the top 10 percent of urban schools nationally (BNOB Education Committee).

SOCIAL CAPITAL: AN EXPLANATION
FOR PUBLIC SCHOOL SUCCESS

"And he said, I saw all Israel scattered upon the hills, as sheep that have no shepherd" (1 Kings 22:17a English Standard Version).

Putnam (2000) defined social capital as the "connections among individuals—social networks and the norms of reciprocity and trustworthiness that arise from them" (Putnam, 2000, 19). These tenets of social capital stretch beyond the mere interpersonal connections with others within our close-knit communities into many facets of our daily lives. He argued that the very central elements of social capital are grounded in the basic notion of "trust and reciprocity" and that social capital has value (Putnam, 2000, 19).

American society, since its inception, has been based upon the fundamental principles that all citizens are entitled to "life, liberty and the pursuit of happiness," as stated in the Declaration of Independence. These fundamental principles are steeped in the notions of liberal democracy and the First Amendment to the U.S. Constitution, the rights of individuals to freely express their opinions and to assemble to express their views. Within this context, the basic tenets of social capital emerged.

Sadly, Americans have seen the attrition of social capital for the Hurricane Katrina victims as many were (and still are) dispersed across this country. We witnessed the attrition of social capital through the mass exodus of students from their homes, schools, communities, as well as the displacement of families, friends, community and social networks. We witnessed the attrition of social capital as Hurricane Katrina victims were forced to live in dehumanizing conditions without the basic necessities of life.

Yet, despite this tragedy, some communities persevered, schools reopened, and life for the victims of Hurricane Katrina continued to hedge forward. This leaves us to consider the answers to questions: How did these schools weather the brutal force of Hurricane Katrina? How did they manage to pull together the resources needed to reopen schools, sustain quality education and maintain community cohesion? How did school administrators and teachers foster positive social and cultural norms in students before as well as after the Hurricane? These matters are central to applying the idea of social capital as a framework for building and sustaining school capacity in the midst of tragedy.

MAINTAINING SCHOOL ACHIEVEMENT
THROUGH SOCIAL CAPITAL

Marjorie W. Lee stated that teachers are "surrogate parents who are instrumental in children's early extra-familial attachments, achievements and social relationships" (Lee, 1991, 3). She also argued that teachers must possess positive parental attributes in order to foster student achievement and social relationships within the school environment. Lee indicated that "teachers who invest their social capital in the lives of their students" transform social capital as a theory to social capital as a practice (Lee, 1991, 4).

Community field theory provides a framework for understanding the role of social capital in educational achievement (Israel, Beautlieu, and Hartless, 2001, 45). The authors maintained that community social capital evolves from community members' investment in local cohesion and solidarity. Thus, the axis of social capital can be seen as a binary method of an explanatory process. This process illuminates the impact of social cohesion and the importance of the interpersonal relationships as individuals connect. Close-knit communal relationships among students in the educational environment greatly influence their level of achievement. Positive social capital also encourages the expression of community support for academic achievement among their members. Thus, the concepts of social cohesion and solidarity can be used to explain educational achievement in the selected public schools that successfully reopened after Hurricane Katrina.

Research abounds in the areas of creating and maintaining social cohesiveness in communities (Putnam, 2000; Lee, 1991; Munn, 2000). However, much of the research on social capital is limited in the area of fostering social capital in schools as a framework for building and sustaining social cohesion and building capacity.

One could argue that from a sociological and educational approach, social capital, indeed, can explain the success of students in certain public schools in New Orleans Parish. Putnam (2000) argued that social capital enables an organization to create the feeling that persons are valued. It gives hope to belief that as a community, we can work together for the betterment of our society.

This premise of social capital is grounded in the conceptual notion that shared cultural beliefs, actions and values among community members provide a solid foundation for internal accountability. Internal accountability maintains the premise that the success or failures of the group are predicated on the efforts and abilities of the group. Thus, a cohesive bond is built and sustained because the relationships between the individuals in the community are based on trust, respect and integrity. These particular attributes help to sustain an organization in the mist of a crisis.

A THEORETICAL FRAMEWORK

According to Baron, Field and Schuller (as cited in Munn, 2000), social capital has been developed as a concept by Boudieu and Coleman to help explain the reproduction of social inequality (Munn, 2000, 172). Coleman's and Putnam's theory of social capital is rooted in the assumption that children's failures or successes in schools can possibly be explained by either the lack of positive social interactions and the lack of access to secure social intimacies, such as family, peer relationships, and a network that promotes quality education as well as educational attainment. Putnam (2000) argues that it is not only human or financial capital, but positive social capital that may determine students' opportunity for academic success.

For the purpose of this chapter, we will anchor this social framework to the theory of social capital. Coleman and Putnam help us relate the central tenets of social capital to the educational situation of victims of Hurricane Katrina. The idea of social capital can help explain a community's willingness to strive to sustain what survived or recreate what was lost. Our sociological understanding of the nature of relationships is predicated on the idea that social intimacy gives significance to individuals. It provides the type of cohesive interaction needed to connect individuals to each other for the greater good of a society. Social capital embraces the notion that *generalized reciprocity* (a term coined by Putnam) is the social fabric into which individuals are woven in daily life (Putnam, 2000).

Putnam argued that social capital employs the "golden rule principle": "Do unto others as you would have them do unto you." To apply these concepts, we must explore and test to determine whether social capital perceptions about the quality of education shifted after Hurricane Katrina. Research was conducted using a threefold approach:

First, we visited New Orleans to observe, firsthand, the effects of the devastation. Freire said that "dehumanization marks not only those whose humanity has been stolen, but also those who have stolen it" (Freire, 2001, 1). Could life observation of the community support this thought?

Second, we collected data on physical damage to elementary and secondary schools and studied how this loss effected students, teachers, other school personnel, and families.

Third, we tried to ascertained the impact of social capital on education, community members' awareness of one another, and the networks that worked. This would help compare social advancement and community issues before and after Katrina.

Three public schools participated in this study. All three have been designated "high performing schools" by the state of Louisiana. All three have a predominately African-American student population. The three schools had selective admissions before Katrina, but they went to open admissions after the disaster in order to gather as many students as possible back into school. Open admissions added challenges, such as lower student attendance, more discipline problems and lower student achievement. To compensate, though, all stakeholders made the value of education and learning a top priority.

A consensus has come from the research at high performing schools. Various studies stress seven important characteristics of these schools:

1. High-performing schools set high standards for student achievement and plan curriculum and assessment based upon those standards.

2. High-performing schools hold teachers and administrators accountable for meeting school goals.
3. High-performing schools create a safe, orderly environment that allows students to concentrate on academics.
4. High-performing schools maximize time spent on instruction.
5. High-performing schools have teachers and administrators who are committed to the philosophy and mission of their schools and who have access to quality professional development that helps them achieve that mission.
6. High-performing schools have high levels of parent and community involvement.
7. High-performing schools have the freedom of flexibility in curriculum design, as well as in making personnel and finance decisions. (U.S. Department of Education's "High Performing Schools Initiative." See at ed.gov/offices/OUS/eval/elem).

METHOD AND ANALYSIS

Twelve teachers and principals at the three schools volunteered to share their perspective regarding the impact of Katrina on general education, school climate, and the general work of teachers and school personnel. At the time of the study, sixty-seven percent of these educators were teachers and eight percent were principals or in other administrative work. Seventy-five percent of the participants were female and remaining 25% male. The educators were from the middle-age range: ages forty-two to forty-seven, 25 percent; forty-eight to fifty-three, 25 percent; and fifty-four to fifty-nine, 25 percent, and the remaining 25percent were ages 41 and younger.

In ethnicity, 83 percent were African Americans and the remaining 17 percent were Caucasians. Although teacher certification data were not requested, in terms of teacher preparation, 75 percent of the respondents hold the master's degree and 17 percent hold the bachelor's degree. Also, 92 percent of the educators have over sixteen years of teaching experience. In this period after Katrina, 58 percent of the educators worked in schools with student populations between 501 and 1,000, while 25 percent in schools with fewer than 500 students, and the rest in schools over 1,000.

The researchers are inclined to believe that, since most of the students are African Americans, culturally relevant instruction practices contribute greatly to the success of these schools. Also, there is likely a strong connection between the level of academic work completed by the teachers and student outcomes.

Due to the unique situation studied—the devastating impact of Katrina that left destroyed communities beyond the imagination of residents—researchers designed a survey to compare the perceptions of educators about the quality of education and social capital before and after Katrina. Therefore, data were collected from educators regarding their perceptions about the period prior to Katrina and in the immediate aftermath. The statements eliciting responses focused on three areas of concern: (1) general education; (2) school climate; and (3) teacher-school personnel issues.

Seven items pertained to perceptions about general education issues of parental support, educational resources, funding, and school environment. General education items were anchored on an excellence scale, in which 1 = Poor, 2 = Fair, 3 = Good, and 4 = Excellent.

Thirteen items covered school climate, including teacher perceptions of class size, professional development, educational support, and school related activities. School climate items were anchored on an agreement scale in which 0 = N/A, 1 = Strongly Disagree, 2 = Somewhat Disagree, 3 = Neither Disagree or Agree, 4 = Somewhat Agree, and 5 = Strongly Agree.

Seven items focused on teacher and school personnel issues, including student tardiness, student attrition, parental support, and enrollment. Teacher and school personnel items were anchored on a problem level scale where 0 = N/A, 1 = No Problem, 2 = Minor Problem, 3 = Moderate Problem, and 4 = Serious Problem.

The survey was given to the educators during the researchers visits to the three schools. Some educators had the opportunity to discuss their teaching experiences prior to Katrina and in the aftermath of Katrina with the researchers before completing the survey.

ANALYSIS: GENERAL EDUCATION

Analysis

Descriptive summaries and paired t-test procedures on educators' pre- and post-Katrina perceptions were computed to determine if a significant shift in attitudes regarding general education occurred. Table 5.1 reveals the results of seven items, but note that the only significant difference [$t_{(10)} = 4.50, p < .01. d = 1.92$] was found in educators' perceptions about extra-curricular activities for students. Educators indicated that extra-curricular activities for students were "good" prior to Katrina but in the aftermath "fair." In addition, the effect size corresponding to this difference suggests a very strong effect (Cohen, 1988).

Of course, this is to be expected. When providing basic education services was a daunting challenge, extra-curricular activities had to be less of a priority. Emphasis was placed on academics and getting students caught up after having been out-of-school for a long period. On the remaining items the per-

Table 5.1. General Education: Comparison on Items of Interest Pre- Post-Katrina

Item	Pre		Post				
	M	SD	M	SD	df	t	p
1. School personnel (administrators, teachers and staff) ability to select textbooks and other instructional materials	2.64	.674	2.45	.820	10	1.49	.17
2. Condition of the school building	2.58	.996	2.17	.835	11	1.82	.10
3. Extra-curricular activities for students	3.00	.632	2.18	.751	10	4.50	.00**
4. Access to school materials and supplies (e.g. paper, pencils, etc.)	2.83	.718	2.50	.798	11	1.77	.10

ception shifts were tenable or not significant. There was a shift in perception regarding the ability to select textbooks and have access to other instructional materials and supplies. There also were perception shifts regarding the condition of school buildings, and funding.

Despite some change in availability, school personnel did continue to select textbooks and receive other instructional materials. To have some degree of control in instruction materials must contribute to confidence and hope. Regarding facility condition, educators reported that buildings were in fair condition when they were reopened for school. This is another good indicator that teaching and learning can be the priority if facility conditions are not optimal. Having to focus on renovations would produce additional stress.

ANALYSIS: SCHOOL CLIMATE

Descriptive summaries and paired t-test procedures on educators' pre- and post-Katrina perceptions were computed to determine if a significant shift in attitudes occurred regarding school climate. Table 5.2 reveals the results of responses to thirteen items. All are tenable, not finding significant differences in the educators' perceptions regarding school climate. Educators somewhat agree to specific school climate items. Time might have effected these perceptions, how soon after Katrina the survey took place. A more substantive understanding of these results can be found in the educator comments.

Table 5.2. School Climate: Comparison on Items of Interest Pre- Post-Katrina

Item	Pre		Post				
	M	SD	M	SD	df	t	p
1. Teachers have reasonable class sizes affording them time to meet the educational needs of all students	3.73	1.49	3.91	1.14	10	-.52	.62
2. Teachers are protected from duties that interfere with their essential role of educating students	4.27	.91	3.82	1.25	10	1.61	.14
3. Adequate and appropriate time is provided for professional development	4.33	.71	4.00	1.23	8	1.41	.20
4. Teachers have "instructional planning time" within the instructional day	3.91	1.04	4.27	1.01	10	-1.49	.17
5. Teachers have adequate professional space to work productively	3.36	1.57	3.45	1.51	10	-.36	.72
6. Teachers have sufficient access to office equipment such as copy machines	3.82	1.25	3.55	1.29	10	1.15	.28
7. Teachers have sufficient access to instructional supplies	4.00	1.00	3.56	1.51	8	1.32	.23
8. Teachers and staff work in a school environment that is safe	3.67	1.41	3.89	1.17	8	-.80	.45
9. Overall, the school has adequate materials, equipment, classrooms, and other facilities for me to do a good job teaching students	3.60	1.43	3.50	1.27	9	.29	.78
10. Teachers have access to student records (e.g. cumulative folder)	3.70	1.06	3.50	1.18	9	1.50	.17
11. Teachers have access to student assessment results/scores (e.g. end-of-grade test, benchmark assessments, etc.)	3.80	1.23	3.60	1.08	9	.69	.51
12. Teachers work together to improve teaching and learning	4.00	1.00	4.36	.67	10	-1.79	.10
13. Teachers are involved with school-related activities, involving student interaction (e.g. field trips, tutoring, club sponsorship) outside of the regular school day	3.55	1.29	3.82	.87	10	-.90	.39

$*p < .05, **p < .01$

ANALYSIS: TEACHERS AND SCHOOL PERSONNEL MATTERS

Descriptive summaries and paired t-test statistical procedure on educators' pre- and post-Katrina perceptions were computed to determine if a significant shift had occurred in attitudes regarding teacher and school personnel. Table 5.3 reveals the results of seven items. Again, all are tenable meaning significant differences in the educators perceptions regarding teacher and school personnel did not occur in the aftermath of Katrina. Nevertheless, the observable results indicate that, for 5 out 7 items [student tardiness, absenteeism, dropout, parent involvement, and parental substance abuse], educators were less positive about the area after the hurricane. For instance, student tardiness and absenteeism shift from borderline to a "moderate problem."

FINDINGS: GENERAL EDUCATION

How did these schools weather the brutal force of Hurricane Katrina? At the time of this research, nine months into the time of rebuilding, a handful of schools were open and available to the researchers. These reopened schools had been considered high performing schools prior to Hurricane Katrina, with select admissions. Students were admitted based on their ability to meet academic requirements. After Katrina, however, these select schools moved to open admissions, accepting all students needing these levels of education.

During the period of shift, the time between the educators' pre-Katrina perceptions and their post-Katrina Perceptions, these schools had been able

Table 5.3. Teacher and School Personnel: Comparison on Items of Interest Pre- Post-Katrina

Item	Pre		Post				
	M	SD	M	SD	df	t	p
1. Student tardiness	2.63	.92	2.88	.64	7	−1.53	.17
2. Student absenteeism	2.75	1.04	3.00	.76	7	−1.53	.17
3. Students dropping out of school	1.38	.74	1.63	1.30	7	−.80	.45
4. Lack of academic challenge	1.71	1.25	1.57	1.27	6	.55	.60
5. Lack of parent involvement	2.71	.76	2.86	.90	6	−1.00	.36
6. Parental alcoholism and/or drug abuse	1.00	.82	1.29	.95	6	−1.55	.17
7. Student enrollment	1.71	1.11	1.43	1.13	6	1.55	.17

$*p < .05, **p < .01$

to return to a high quality of education. They held in place high-quality staff who were equipped to meet the needs of the students during this time. There was not a significant shift in perceptions about the schooling experience after the storm. For example, the teachers at the selected schools noted that they had access to school materials and supplies. In fact, the participants in the study rated their response to this question as very good. Also, in terms of the condition of the building, the participants in the study noted that the building was in fair condition. However, there was some variance in responses to this particular item, as noted by the standard deviation. Conversely, the results were tenable in the sense that the same observations were made about the period before the disruption.

So, what does this tell us about sustaining schooling in the wake of such an event? The evidence of these relatively successful schools is that support resources and systems are important to returning facilities to their capacity. This means that local education agencies (LEAs) should create a plan of action for providing classroom instruction support materials needed by teachers and students. They also need to identify alternate sites for schools in the event that the pre-existing building is destroyed. Plans must be in place to outfit these emergency facilities with the technology needed to support the retrieval of school documents.

The second research question presented in this study reveals how the selected school communities were able to pull together the social capital needed to reopen schools. During the shifting period, the participants noted that they were able to work together to improve the teaching and learning environment. In fact, participants of the study indicated that there was little difference in the amount of quality time they were able to spend planning for instruction and reflecting on the teaching and learning process with their colleagues. This in itself is a significant finding in terms of the lack of difference in the participants' perceptions regarding this issue. One can explain this phenomenon as social capital.

The participants in the study have a strong positive connection to each other, building social cohesion, and strong solidarity towards the school and its environment. Therefore, this connection sustains and motivates staff during a difficult time of rebuilding programs. The survey participants are able to work together to find and share the resources needed to continue to foster high quality education for students. Teachers and students are strongly connected to each other and to the school.

Regarding the third research question, how these educators were able to maintain social cohesiveness, the data reports that they maintained social contacts and connections with the community. The participants noted that there was not a significant difference in their participation in community events. Lee (1991) posits that a stabilizing element of a community's social capital is its ability to maintain social cohesion and solidarity during a crisis. This ability to maintain strong bonds and positive social capital has allowed the schools in this study, to continuously provide a high-quality educational program and to share social capital among its community members.

We infer that school administrators and teachers sustain high academic quality, social cohesion, and a "sense" of community through pre-existing social connections. The research purports that school administrators' and teachers' perceptions of community practices and social interconnectedness did not shift.

LESSONS LEARNED: IMPLICATIONS FROM PRACTICE

The lessons learned from the selected schools show that the difficulties in overcoming disaster can seem insurmountable, yet it is possible to press on. The schools in this study seem to be models for maintaining high quality education and solidarity in the midst of the "storm." These schools put into practice the theoretical constructs noted in this chapter. Creating educational environments where students and staff members feel connected to the common goal is central to the sustaining school achievement. This type of practice illustrates the researchers' premise that social capital is needed if schools are to nurture a caring atmosphere with strong social cohesion and sustained program quality.

Public schools must work towards building community with their external as well as internal publics. After the hurricane, it was pre-existing connection with the schools' external publics that contributed to the community's interest in rebuilding their school. Therefore, it is important to recognize the collective efforts of community members and their willingness to rebuild the infrastructure that made their schools symbols of hope for a better tomorrow.

Lastly, after the devastation of Katrina, the educators, parents and some politicians focused on re-opening schools. The educators went into a survival mode and focused on the essentials of ensuring that students were given the opportunity to learn. It is in this sense of community that we witness the human spirit at work, a desire to survive, to continue, to rebuild and to sustain excellence, even in the midst of tragedy. The researchers appreciated the opportunity to witnessed the survival, and to tell the story of successful schools.

REFERENCES

Bring New Orleans Back (BNOB) Committee, online at bringneworleansback.org/.
Cawelti, G. (2000). "Portrait of a benchmark school." *Educational Leadership,* 57.5: 42–44.

Charles A. Dana Center, University of Texas at Austin (1999). "Hope for urban education: A study of nine high performing, high poverty urban elementary schools." Washington, DC: U.S. Department of Education, Planning and Evaluation Service. Retrieved December 6, 2003 at ed.gov/offices/OUS/eval/elem.

Cohen, J. (1988). *Statistical power analysis for the behavioral sciences,* 2d ed. Hillsdale, NJ: Lawrence Erlbaum.

Democracy Now interview by Amy Goodman with Joe DeRose, Communication Director for the United Teachers of New Orleans. June 20, 2006, pp. 1–6. http://www.Democracynow.org/article.pl?sid

Dekker, Paul, and Eric Uslaner (2001). *Social Capital and Participation in Everyday Life.* New York: Routledge.

Dyson, Michael Eric. *Come Hell or High Water: Hurricane Katrina and the Color of Disaster.* New York: Basic, 2006.

Franklin, John Hope (2005). *Mirror to America: The Autobiography of John Hope Franklin.* New York: Farrar, Straus & Giroux.

Glidden, H. G. (1999). "Breakthrough schools: Characteristics of low-income schools that perform as though they were high-income schools." *ERS Spectrum, Journal of School Research and Information,* 17.2: 21–26.

Hill, P.& Hannaway, J. (January 2006). The Urban Institute. The future of public education in new orleans, pp. 1–12. http://www.urban.org

Hopkins, M. S. (1999). "Effective School Practices: What Works." Paper presented at the 1999 International Conference on Effective Schools, Houston, Texas.

Irvine, Jacqueline (2002). *In Search of Wholeness: African American Teachers and Their Culturally Specific Classroom Practices.* New York: Palgrave.

Israel, G., Beaulieu, L., Hartless, G. (2001), The Influence of Family and Community Social Capital on Educational Achievement. Rural Sociology, 66(1), 43–68

Lee, Marjorie W. (1991). "Social Capital An Investment of 'Self' In Young Children." In Roy Evans, ed. *Early Child Development and Care.* 73.3–18.

Lein, L. (1997). "Successful Texas School-wide Program: Research Study Results, School Profiles, Voices of Practitioners and Parents, Self Study and Planning Guide [and] Suggestions for Technical Assistance Providers," clearinghouse no. RC020983. ERIC Document Reproduction Service, no. ED 406 084.

Louisiana Department of Education (LDE), at louisianaschools.net.

Munn, Pamela (2000). *Social Capital, Schools and Exclusions. In Baron, Stephen, Field, John and Schuller, Tom. Social Capital Critical Perspectives.* Oxford: Oxford University Press.

New Orleans Public School System, at nops.k12.la.us.

New Orleans Public Schools. "Recovery School District Legislatively Required Plan," June 2006.

Putnam, R. (2000). Bowling Alone: The Collapse and Revival of American Community. New York: Simon and Schuster.

Chapter Six

Katrina Aftermath: Students from Historically Black Universities and Their Perceptions of Social Consciousness

Wanda B. Coneal and Sylvia R. Carey

Student-led demonstrations against government sanctioned discriminatory American practices and laws have not been as prevalent as they were in the 50s and 60s. However, after Hurricane Katrina, a catastrophic Category 3 storm, swept through New Orleans in August 2005 with sustained winds of 120 mph, students attending Historically Black Colleges and Universities (HBCUs) in the area experienced the effects of racial and income disparities. As the college students were making new friends, conversing with old acquaintances about their summer happenings, purchasing textbooks, and preparing to attend orientation activities, Hurricane Katrina was quickly approaching the "Big Easy" as New Orleans is affectionately called. As learners readied for the fall semester, they had no idea that this oncoming natural disaster would become a defining moment in their lives. Hurricane Katrina, which would leave three levees virtually useless and thus flood 80% of the city, provided the impetus for the treatment of the city's poorest and disproportionately Black population to be shown around the world in the most dehumanizing of circumstances (Internet resource). Beyond dead bodies floating in the water and individuals having neither food nor water, the lack of immediate assistance from the local, state, and federal governments proved most disappointing to the college students. It was how poor Americans were disrespected and referred to as "refugees" by the media, which intimates that victims did not have a "home." Hence, the poor were treated as though they were not Americans and did not receive the expected privileges that accompany citizenship in the wealthiest nation in the world.

This observance compelled some HBCU students to challenge themselves to define, or in some cases redefine, "social consciousness," "activism," and "community service." The purpose of this work was to determine how the issues of racism and poverty, which were made evident in the aftermath of Hurricane Katrina, impacted HBCU students' level of social consciousness, and commitment to using their education to become activists and community service volunteers. As college educators, we believed that it would be imperative to learn how aware HBCU college students are of society's ills and their plans to improve the community at local, state, national, and global levels.

BACKGROUND OF STUDENT ACTIVISM

On February 1, 1960, Ezell Blair, Franklin Eugene McCain, Joseph Alfred McNeil, and David L. Richmond, four students from North Carolina Agricultural and Technical College took their places in history when they waited for service at the F. W. Woolworth's lunch counter (Chafe, 1980). Other change agents of that time included women from prestigious Bennett College who participated in sit-ins, demonstrated, and who were arrested for resisting the norms of a racist society (Brown, 1998; Chafe, 1980). College students defied systems of racial oppression in North Carolina as well as in other cities of the United States. For instance, in California, community college students Huey P. Newton and Bobby G. Seale formed the Black Panther Party in 1966 (Monaghan, 2007). Although images of the student sit-ins and those of the Black Panthers may have varying connotations for some and may even be perceived to be at opposite ends of the continuum, each of the aforementioned student-organized groups attempted to gain respect for themselves and for others who were treated unfairly.

Levine and Hirsch (1991) suggested that after three major periods—World War I, World War II, Vietnam—student personal preoccupation increased. The scholars characterized "personal preoccupation" as demonstrating:

> . . . *diminished student activism; more centrist politics; increased isolationism and reduced international concern; rising interest in social activity, Greek membership, and alcohol consumption; greater liberalism in matters of personal freedom; increased church participation; reduced intellectual orientation; and more concern with the material aspects of life* (p. 126).

Levine (1980) initially introduced the term "Titantic Ethic" to describe students who did not believe that conditions in the world were improving, but rather, worsening. As the "ship" was sinking, these individuals wanted to have the best of things as they went down with the "ship," a term that could represent the world, United States, or any other entity. As such, this attitude is further described as "community ascendancy" and "individual ascendancy" which are negatively correlated and constantly changing. While persons who focused on the community then they do not emphasize self, and vice-versa (Levine & Wilson, 1979).

Students who demonstrated in the 1960s fought for equal rights by taking to the streets and by vocalizing publicly their protests rather than by enduring often lengthy court processes. Atty. Thurgood Marshall of the NAACP's Legal Defense Fund and Dr. Martin Luther King, Jr., both recognized the important role and visibility that college students brought to the war for justice (Flowers, DATE??). By refusing to go to the courts, which tended to sanction Jim Crow laws, students ensured that their collective voices and concerns were heard. Their fearlessness and impatience certainly propelled the struggle to the national stage, and consequently, advance their cause for civil rights.

Prior to Katrina, Louisiana's poor struggled to live the American Dream. Louisiana officials reported that 30% of its children lived in poverty, and tied with Mississippi to have the highest infant mortality rate, 10.3 deaths per 1,000 cases (Alter, 2005, p. 47). Lack of resources is not new in this state, and the effects of poverty, i.e. substandard education, lack of quality housing, high unemployment, and insufficient health care, were evident in New Orleans.

The majority of participants in this study were able to recognize the faces of poor human beings and seemed unable to understand the governments' failure to react and rescue those who were unable to evacuate the city before Hurricane Katrina arrived. A year later, the study's participants were continuing to grapple with the reality of the slow response from all three levels—local, state, federal—of government. Moreover, they appeared curious as to whether or not the response time would have been the same if the majority of Katrina's victims would have been wealthy and white. Would economically influential persons have been bussed to the Superdome and forced to remain there with overflowing toilets from the bathrooms? Would powerful decision-makers been kept abreast of the next course of action if they had found themselves temporarily homeless? Would persons who earned 6-figure salaries been stopped by another town's armed police officers from entering their community? Would residents of exclusive neighborhoods still be living in trailers, more than 12 months after the storm? Certainly, such issues have caused the 20 African American students in this study to pause and grapple with the effects of racism and poverty.

The following research questions guided this research:

1. How has Katrina impacted college students' ideal of social consciousness?
2. How has Katrina impacted college students' commitment to activism?
3. How has Katrina impacted college students' commitment to community service?

THEORETICAL FRAMEWORK

Giddings' model of social consciousness underpins this work. This model ". . . was adapted from Gadow's application of Hegel's dialectical reasoning process" (Giddings, 2005, p. 227). Rather than having sequential stages that must be completely satisfied prior to moving to the next phase, this framework allowed the three social consciousness positions—acquired, awakened, expanded—to "co-exist." Consequently, an individual, depending upon the issue, may be in more than one position simultaneously. Another noteworthy quality of Giddings' framework was that each social consciousness position is equal in value; therefore, reaching one position of social consciousness was not necessarily an indicator of maturity (Giddings, 2005).

Characteristics of the Giddings' (2005, pp. 228–233) three social consciousness positions are as follows:

Acquired Social Consciousness

- Refers to the dominant mainstream paradigm;
- Consciously hides differences that are not accepted by mainstream paradigm;
- Rarely questions authority on what is right or wrong treatment;
- Learns rules that society has established in order to receive perks and benefits of belonging;
- Fails to see self as a victim or as being marginalized;
- Survives by not publicly acknowledging wrongs but by ensuring that rules are followed.

Awakened Social Consciousness

- Evaluates society's rules and is not fearful of disagreeing with them;
- Becomes aware of disparities in treatment and may offer alternatives;
- May resist perceived oppressor either directly or indirectly;
- Survives by actively challenging "normal."

Expanded Social Consciousness

- Identifies strongly with own culture;
- Realizes that acceptance in mainstream culture is could change;
- Constantly revises how to respond to changing contexts and situations in the dominant culture;
- Chooses carefully how to respond to stimuli rather than reacts impulsively;

- Acknowledges that oppression and privilege exist and that he/she may even benefit because individuals "other than from mainstream" cultures are oppressed;
- Works with mainstream society and attempts to teach them about others who are members of their marginalized group;
- Lives between two worlds—own culture and mainstream.

The distinct characteristics of the three social consciousnesses adequately described our participants' feelings and actions. Through observations, survey responses, and interviews, it became clear that many of the college participants were wrestling with the realities of life before Katrina with those after Katrina. In this same vein, they were determining what, if any, action that needed to originate from their own devices.

METHODOLOGY

Twelve college students participated in this qualitative study. Because we wanted to give voice to individuals who had actually witnessed the effects of Hurricane Katrina, it was imperative that we used a research methodology that permitted them to express their perceptions and thoughts.

SAMPLING

Through convenience sampling, we selected 20 participants who met our criteria of being an undergraduate at an institution of higher education in New Orleans when Hurricane Katrina entered the city and having an earned grade point average of 3.0 or higher. (Myriad programs of study were represented in this study.) In order to accommodate their varied class and part-time job schedules, the researchers of this study concluded that convenience sampling was the most feasible strategy to use.

DEMOGRAPHICS

There were 12 participants—8 women and 4 men. Before Katrina, 58% performed community service that included building houses with Habitat Humanity, preparing lunch in an alcoholic-recovering shelter, mentoring and tutoring elementary school-aged students, and painting a public New Orleans' school. Eight percent volunteered at a college library, and 33% had not participated in any community-service projects prior to Katrina. Even though they were all members of campus organizations, whether at the university or at their graduating high schools, all had not been involved in their self-defined "meaningful" community-service projects.

DATA COLLECTION

Before semi-structured interviews were conducted, the 12 participants completed an open-ended survey. Although the interviews took on a conversational format, the questions from the interview protocol were addressed by the undergraduates and the focus of this study was not lost. To ensure trustworthiness in accordance with Lincoln and Guba's techniques (1985), we established credibility of data by triangulating information, collecting referential adequacy materials, and performing peer debriefings. Additionally, we researchers ensured that all questions on the interview protocol would be asked in the same manner and format. Because we are individuals, it was imperative that we agreed to be as uniformed and unemotional as possible while interviewing because it is not uncommon for participants to respond to the body language and subconscious clues of researchers.

DATA ANALYSIS

Research questions guided both our investigation and data analysis. Utilizing the concepts associated with grounded theory and open-coding, we developed analytic categories by determining the emerging patterns and themes that aligned with our research questions (Berg, 2004). To ensure that we did not misinterpret our findings, we discussed in-depth survey results and taped (and transcribed) interviews. In our discourse, three pertinent questions were used to reach logico-inductive conclusions (Vierra and Pollock, 1988):

1. What do I know?
2. How can I be sure this is accurate?
3. What other explanations are possible?

The researchers of this study discussed the data to be certain that we had not been influenced by media reports but rather heard from the college students, our participants. To be certain that we not misrepresent the students, we made students aware that follow-up conversations would be necessary, especially if we needed clarification. The talks were informal and, as much as possible, in comfortable settings in order for participants to relax and speak from their hearts. Indeed, it was not our intentions to incite but to capture truth from the students' perspectives.

LIMITATIONS AND STRENGTHS

Time constraints for observations and interviewing proved to be the greatest limitation to this study. During our visit to New Orleans during the end of the spring semester, we were competing with conflicting class schedules and part-time jobs. While we, the two researchers, were physically unable to observe each participant as fully as we had hoped, we ensured that we conducted at least two face-to-face interviews and had opportunities to follow-up after we left New Orleans. I believe that more rich data could have been collected if we had been able to actually witness more of the subjects' day-to-day lives both within and outside the classroom environment.

Despite limitations, we are confident that this study will contribute to the literature about the aftermath of Hurricane Katrina. The majority of published reports do not include how the storm has impacted HBCU students. This qualitative investigation adds to the conversation in terms of how this experience has influenced how they will use their education to impact the community.

FINDINGS

The purpose of this work was to determine how the issues of racism and poverty, which were made evident in the aftermath of Hurricane Katrina, impacted HBCU students' level of social consciousness, and commitment to using their education to become activists and community—service volunteers. The research questions that guided this qualitative study were as follows:

1. How has Katrina impacted college students' ideal of social consciousness?
2. How has Katrina impacted college students' commitment to activism?
3. How has Katrina impacted college students' commitment to community service?

The study examined how HBCU students changed from before the hurricane to after and their projections for the future. Utilizing qualitative methodology allowed participants to voice their concerns about each question posed to them in the semi-structured interviews and on the open-ended surveys.

Through focused conversation, the data that we collected and analyzed generated the following conclusions.

SOCIAL CONSCIOUSNESS

Using a 3-position framework of social consciousness that Gadow's (1995) modification of Hegel's dialectical reasoning, we were able to understand better how HBCU students exhibited social consciousnesses traits as they lived through a range of emotional states. The phases of this model are non-hierarchical; therefore, individuals may find themselves, simultaneously, in more than one position of the framework. As well, individuals may have experienced the same event but will react differently, as this student points out:

> *I was really excited at first when I cam back . . . . I thought everyone would be as, you know, as radical as me. I really thought that the whole Hurricane [issue] would have exposed the blatant institutional racism in the city. And, I thought that the [university], you know, I always remembered us being a fairly conscious university. I really figured that students would really be ready to move, like students have moved in the 50s, 60s, and 70s. But when I got here, I found that everyone was basically complacent. But somehow the media industrial complex had already compromised our minds and to just coming back and being complacent.*

ACQUIRED SOCIAL CONSCIOUSNESS

The first position of the social consciousness model is essentially when one denies that others either may benefit or be disadvantaged because of physical and ethnic attributes. Though you may witness unequal treatment, you do not perceive that people in positions of power and authority may have prejudices. Rather, you may counter that these instances signal "just how it is" or people bought these things upon themselves. This position is evident when people accept life "as is" and do not make an effort to fight against such policies and practices. This especially the case when these interruptions do not negatively impact them.

Some participants said that they believed that people chose to ignore warnings to evacuate because of unwise decision-making rather race and income. Katie stated:

> *. . . two of my uncles live in New Orleans. And one uncle was able to evacuate and come to Mississippi, nearby where I live. But my other uncle actually had*

to be rescued off the roof of his house. So, he-he doesn't like to talk about the situation much but we worried about him. But, I don't know anybody that was in the Dome. I wish he had been in the Dome. I wish he had been evacuated. He was one of those people that didn't think that the storm would do anything . . . that he could survive it.

Besides Katie, other participants mentioned that they knew of New Orleans' residents who simply did not believe meteorologists because they had been warned in previous years to seek safer shelter, and storms turned out to be less horrific than predicted. On the other hand, some residents wanted to leave the city but either did not have anywhere to go or did not have the resources to leave. Regardless of the reason, the majority of participants made it clear that before viewing media coverage of the aftermath, they simply placed the onus on the adults who decided to remain. Or, if they did not have the resources, if they had planned better for their financial futures, they would have had viable options. Their mindset corresponded with their desire to "make something of themselves" and to accomplish their dreams even in the face of surmounting societal prejudices.

Everywhere I travel, I try to represent myself very articulately and knowledge-able and stuff like that and just because, that is a myth. And, I understand that, you know, by being Black and everything, there is already a negative connota-tion associate with it. And, a lot of times, it's not their fault [European Ameri-cans] . . . that's just the country that we live in. And, it's just going to happen so that's why I always try to make it an effort to try to represent my school and rep-resent HBCUs the best that I can. So, yeah, I think I did dispel a lot of myths.

This young man is attempting to "disprove" myths that European American may have about African Americans by being mainstreamed and representing himself in the best light. He is also excusing them from taking responsibility for their role in the inequalities of our country. Rather than holding them accountable and even being angry, he sees his role as teaching them that African Americans are articulate and not what they have heard. He appears to be a self-proclaimed ambassador for educated African Americans and for HBCUs.

HIGHER EDUCATION

Seeking undergraduate degrees was a way to acceptance in mainstream society, financial freedom and achieving the American dream. One participant declared, "I understand that in order for me to live a successful and happy life,

I needed a college degree." In the same vein, a second student recalled his reasons, "Education is the way to have financial stability later on in life." Being a role model was another reason for seeking a degree, "My reasons for deciding to earn a 4-year degree consist of: being the first person in my family to attend college; becoming a role model for my younger siblings; and the goal to become an attorney or a politician." Another expressed similar sentiments, "I felt that a minimum of a 4-year degree is necessary to even make a way for myself. A high school diploma equates to hardly nothing so this was mandatory."

> *After Katrina, the reason for higher education seemed to change or at least re-confirmed as to the influence of a college degree. Katrina did not change my view of what education is. What it did? It did make me understand that educa-tion is very key, and not just for myself, but I mean for everyone who was at-tending the university. I thought that Katrina was a wake-up call and that we all needed to be aware of what was going on and especially because we go to school in New Orleans. . . . But my long-term career goals were to be to work with a government agency probably local, I would say, because that was my first step [as to] how I would give back to the community, give back to my country, give back to people who have helped me get to my level of education. I thought that was the first way for me to kind of give back. . . . I think that Katrina just made me realize that look, I have—I have a vision, and I can work with people. I need to take back the leadership role. Katrina did . . . it did motivate me. You know it's unfortunate that it took such an event to-to kind of wake me up . . .*

AWAKENED SOCIAL CONSCIOUSNESS

Katrina served as a "wake-up call" for these college students to use their ed-ucation to become leaders. Their initial reasons for advancing in their career fields seemed was no longer about advancing for individual gain but also to inspire their communities with hope and solutions. The *awakened* position is acknowledging that there are disparities and injustices in society that need to be challenged. One who is *awakened* may no longer justify why some are op-pressed and others are privileged because "that is just the way it is." Rather, they are now questioning inequalities and wanting others to "wake-up." In terms of resistance, they may resist, either directly or indirectly, powerful au-thorities or the organization that they believe culpable for the oppression. Whether resisting directly or indirectly, in this position, people become angry when they realize the disparities within society. One student said,

> *I don't understand how they [United States in Iraq] are helping to build places overseas, but there are places, the Ninth Ward, still devastated. I can't under-*

stand that in my head. How could they not provide assistance for us? And they just say, 'Okay. You know we're going to help you.' I see small things being done, but I feel like there's a greater cause. Some people think that the music here is important. Well, the people have nowhere to live, why do we need the music?

One student who believed that the government and the American public had forgotten about New Orleans stated:

I believe that if it had been more Caucasian people, they would have responded faster and in a better way besides keeping people in the Superdome and bussing them to Texas. And, I just think much more assistance would have been provided. . . . Yes, I feel moments of anger whenever I visit other college campuses or see other college students and whenever I watch the news and see new reports of other things, I feel like they've forgotten us. I feel like they no longer think about how this was really a life-changing thing . . . how long it will affect all of our lives and how we still struggle with Katrina every day. I'm angry at the fact that basically their lives are still going on when our lives were, our lives are still not on the, on the same pace that they once were or that they would be. I'm angry about it.

Channeling the anger is significant in the *awakened* position. Some participants planned to attend a march with the Rev. Jesse Jackson and the Rev. Al Sharpton that addressed the manner in which the poor, and disproportionate number of African Americans, were treated. One participant, who aspires to become a politician was angry and spearheaded a student group to stand for those without a voice.

I was angry. One I was angry at-at just the overall situation that happened. Then, I was angry at how people were treated here, and it really reflected the racism that still exists in America. I was angry that people weren't getting the help they desperately needed. We were able to organize over 30 volunteers for the march with Jesse Jackson.

EXPANDED SOCIAL CONSCIOUSNESS

In this position, the person makes a choice on how to handle injustice. Though he may not participate in a march to express his views, he will resist within the system to demonstrate his disapproval. Though he is resisting, he is not attempting necessarily to dissociate himself from mainstream society or from the privileges of his own status. Rather than boycotting, which he may deem as activism, he may tutor students from poor neighborhoods or volunteer his expertise under the umbrella of "community service."

Community Service vs. Activism

The majority of college participants in this study are working with various groups to assist in rebuilding New Orleans. Some are building houses with Habitat for Humanity, tutoring in elementary schools, serving as a Big Brother/Big Sister mentor, and joining church and community-centered organizations and groups. Others would like to use their current level of knowledge to assist with the rebuilding.

As an engineering major, I feel that I could one day apply my assistance on the rebuilding of the levees and making sure that they stay sturdy and modern enough to stand up to, you know, the worst changes in climate, and you know, different factor that, you know, affect the city every day. I feel that I could assist with that.

Several students also shared their views on why serving their community is a new priority:

I guess it makes me want to have a kinder heart not to judge people because you never know what could happen to you. I think, you know, my long-term goal, I think, is probably to work in a community agency. So, I mean helping people is basically my ultimate goal.

   I just recently went to the State of the Black Union with Tavis smiley and that was one of the most inspiring things. It showed me that just because you're in the media or you're working for communications doesn't mean that you have to be all about yourself and that you don't have to just work in their [European Americans] world. You can also work in your own community. I think the things that he's doing is wonderful, and that hopefully in some ways, I can start my own program like that to help the community around me and also work with my own people.

DISCUSSION AND RECOMMENDATIONS

The purpose of this work was to determine how the issues of racism and poverty, which were made evident in the aftermath of Hurricane Katrina, impacted HBCU students' level of social consciousness, and commitment to using their education to become activists and community service volunteers. The participants in this study evidenced the various positions of the social consciousness framework by how they expressed their perceptions, emotions, and plans for the future.

Recommendations

• University administrators and faculty must provide continued nurture and guidance on how to use their knowledge to impact positively the city.

- Student organizations could participate in policy-making and strategizing sessions and be recognized as contributors to ongoing conversations with politicians, engineers, businesses leaders, educators, etc.
- Faculty could incorporate project-based and community-based learning opportunities that actually bring students face-to-face with Katrina victims. They should be able to put a face with the statistical data.
- Students need to have dialogue about their feelings that will include solutions to rebuild the community. These sessions would allow students to vent as well as to take ownership of the issues.

REFERENCES

Astin, A. W. (1993). An empirical typology of college students. *Journal of College Student Development*, 34, 36–46.

Beutel, A., & Johnson, M. (2004). Gender and prosocial values during adolescence: A research note. *Sociological Quarterly*, 45(2), 379–393.

Cress, C. M. (2001). Developmental outcomes of college students' involvement in leadership. *Journal of College Student Development*, 42, 15–27.

DeSwaan, A. (2000). Elite perceptions of the poor: Reflections for a comparative research project. *Current Sociology*, 28(1), 43.

Flowers, D. B. (2004). The launching of the student sit-in movement: The role of black women at Bennett College. *Journal of African American History*, 90(1–2), 52–63.

Giddings, L. S. (2005). A theoretical model of social consciousness. *Advances in Nursing Science*, 28(3), 224–239.

Herbeck, J. (2004). Awakening social consciousness. *Book Links*, 13(4), 6.

Shelby, T. (2003). Ideology, racism, and critical social theory. *Philosophical Forum*, 34(2), 153–188.

Weakliem, D. L. (2002). The effects of education on political opinions: An international study. *International Journal of Public Opinion Research*, 14(2), 141–157.

Weis, L. & Fine, M. (2001). Extraordinary conversations in public schools. *International Journal of Qualitative Studies in Education*, 14(4), 497–527.

Yates, M. (1998). The development of social responsibility as a meaning making process: The role of schools. *Human Development*, 41(4), 279–282.

Chapter Seven

Technology Engineering Educational Solutions for the Hurricane Katrina Region

James E. Osler II

INTRODUCTION

The advent of computers has greatly changed education. This change has been further enhanced by the development of the internet and interactive programming courseware that aids and enhances instruction. Computers and the internet have allowed educators to broaden their horizons and extend their ability to reach, train, and teach both colleagues and students. The ability to reach teachers and learners by providing digital educational resources can be vital in aiding those living in regions devastated by natural disasters in re-establishing their learning environments. The goal of this chapter is to provide solutions that have been implemented and are being created for the residents of the United States who are living in the Hurricane Katrina region.

THE PROBLEM: THE CURRENT STATE OF EDUCATION IN THE REGION

As of February 1, 2006 Linda Jacobson of Education Week reported the following: "As students displaced by Hurricanes Katrina and Rita continue returning to their home school districts in Louisiana and Mississippi, tens of thousands remain scattered elsewhere in those states, in nearby states, and across the nation. Five months after schools began rolling out the welcome mat for families fleeing New Orleans and other storm-ravaged communities, officials are still working out graduation requirements, cost reimbursements, and other questions affecting students who can't return home yet, or who are making a new home.

According to the most recent data provided to Education Week by state educa-tion departments, Louisiana had the highest number of students—105,000—at-tending schools in the state that are not their home schools" (Jacobson, 2006). Thus, solutions are needed to provide educational opportunities to students and educational resources to teachers who remain in the hurricane ravaged region.

CURRENT SOLUTIONS: THE U.S. DEPARTMENT OF EDUCATION'S SUPPORTING AMERICANS AFFECTED BY HURRICANE KATRINA

United States Department of Education Secretary Margaret Spellings has stated the following in the initiative on Supporting Americans Affected by Hurricane Katrina by the U.S. Department of Education, "The children af-fected by Hurricane Katrina need a sense of structure and normalcy. And they need our support. We must not let this tragedy disrupt their education. We will work to help states and communities welcome these students and get them en-rolled into schools as quickly as possible." The Initiative to Support Ameri-cans Affected by Hurricane Katrina has the following goals and statements:

Meeting the Needs of Students and Schools

- *President Bush has directed federal agencies to do everything in their power to save lives and assist Americans affected by Hurricane Katrina.*
- *The U.S. Department of Education is working with states and communities as they welcome the children displaced by Hurricane Katrina and get them enrolled into schools as quickly as possible. In the wake of this tragedy, it is important that we keep our commitment to provide every child with a quality education.*
- *The Department's Assistant Secretary of Elementary and Secondary Edu-cation, Henry Johnson, formerly Mississippi's state superintendent of edu-cation, and other Department officials are working in the Gulf Coast region with State and local education officials to determine the full range of stu-dent-related and school-related needs.*
- *The Department of Education launched Hurricane Help for* Schools (www .ed.gov/katrina) to *serve as a nationwide clearinghouse resource for schools to post their needs and for Americans to help displaced students. More and more matches are made every day between schools needing help and companies, organizations, schools and individuals willing to help across the U.S.*

- *The Department continues to follow up and coordinate with the more than 50 national education organizations that attended a meeting with Secretary Spellings to determine other ways to coordinate and deploy resources.*
- *Department employees have joined the effort and are participating in Project Backpack collecting supplies to send to children in affected areas.*

Marshalling Federal Education Resources to Assist Americans Affected by the Hurricane

- The Department is working closely with Congress to marshal federal education resources to best meet the needs of children, families and schools affected by this tragedy.
- The Department provided guidance to colleges and universities to enable them to admit students from impacted institutions in a way that ensures these students continue to receive federal student aid.
- Student loan borrowers living in affected areas will be automatically granted a forbearance of payments for at least three months, and deadlines for a number of the Department's higher education programs have been extended until at least December 1, 2005.
- On a case-specific basis, Secretary Spellings and the Department will be considering accommodations to provisions of the *No Child Left Behind Act* for affected states.

Good Neighbors: Americans Reaching Out to Help

Communities across the United States are reaching out to those affected by Hurricane Katrina, including:

- In a nationwide effort, numerous states have opened their doors and waived residency requirements for displaced K-12 students.
- Many universities and colleges across the country have agreed to accept students enrolled in Gulf Coast-area universities and to reduce tuition and fees for the fall semester.

DEFINING TECHNOLOGY ENGINEERING AS AN EDUCATIONAL SOLUTION TO PROVIDE OPPORTUNITY AND RESOURCES TO STUDENTS AND TEACHERS IN THE REGION

"Technology Engineering" is both an interactive process and an instruction strategy integrates and seamlessly infuses interactive technology, collaborative methods, and discovery learning with content and curriculum. The author developed this terminology to provide an empowering and effective teaching strategy that takes advantage of the many varied modes of instruction offered by technology in the "Digital Information Age." Technology Engineering is the combination of two distinct yet interrelated concepts combined together as a whole. "Technology" which is the use of the tools and machines that help to solve problems and "Engineering" which is is the application of technology to solve human problems. The two concepts combined create the term "Technology Engineering" which is the product of the two "sets" of knowledge fused together and applied to specifically to instruction (Osler, 2005).

An example of the use of Technology Engineering is the following: Interactive Hypermedia Learning Modules and Asynchronous Learning Networks: Course Management Systems vigorously applied to the course curriculum and is embedded into the structure of the learning environment. These varied modes instruction can be combined with effective Collaborative Learning Strategies to create a dynamic "Cognitive Economy" in the learning environment that delivers the course content in a way that aids the learner in acquiring knowledge (Osler, 2006). In addition, this new philosophy creates an environment that allows the student to take advantage of their multiple learning styles while delivering a high locus of learner control. Thus, the instructor promotes community and discovery, which in turn, can greatly affect the way in which learners retain content.

Interactivity and Collaboration are required and inherent components of the Technology Engineering Philosophy; the courses that are taught with this philosophy can use online interactive networking programs (Asynchronous Learning Networks or ALNs many of which are now used as Course Management Systems) in conjunction with interactive and dynamic teaching techniques (such as Authentic Tasks, Instructional Design Models, Teambuilding Techniques, Culturally Dynamic Teaching Methods, Collaborative Projects, Learner-Based Tools, Product Based Learning, Hands-On Strategies, and Assignments that include Discovery Learning). This infusion of technology with interactive and dynamic teaching methods creates an enriching experience, innovation in the learning environment, and strong sense of ownership and community within the course by both students and faculty (Osler, 2005).

Technology Engineered course shells can provide both instructors and learners with dynamic and extensive tools that allow them the freedom to build connections, actively collaborate, and express thoughts, ideas, perspectives, views, and opinions (Osler, 2006).

Examples of computer—based tools that foster this type of intellectual academic freedom are:

- Virtual Chatting
- Videostreaming
- Real Time Interaction

- Virtual Recording and Replay
- Discussion Forums
- Media Broadcasting: News Feeds (RSS) and Internet Radio
- Email
- Teleconferencing
- Voice Over Internet Protocol
- Message Boards
- eJournals
- Graphic User Interfaces
- Webpages
- ePortfolios
- Virtual Development Tools; and
- Interactive Learning Environments

The use of the aforementioned tools along with course design principles that encourage, facilitate, and promote discovery, positive reinforcement, interactivity, shared experiences, active and ongoing dialogue, and a high locus of control, can create a sense of togetherness and empowerment by both faculty and students enrolled in the course. Thus, the instructor can thereby increase interest in the subject matter, encourage learning, and continue to develop a global sense of ownership that is both empowering and innovative. This is the ultimate goal of Technology Engineering.

THE FOUNDATIONS OF TECHNOLOGY ENGINEERING

Previous work by the author involved the development of effective Interactive Ergonomic Learner—Based Tools and their seamless infusion into course content. Inquiry in this arena led interesting questions such as: "Is it possible to combine subject matter and interactive tools to increase subject matter retention and transfer?" Results of this research went well past the initial expectations. Added outcomes included comments that were lively, engaging, enjoyable and unexpectedly empowering for both students and faculty. Further study and attempts to rationalize, add meaning, and a more global structure to the process yielded a new terminology for this particular method of instruction. Results of this new method of instruction determined that it had an unexpectedly powerful outcome.

The outcome of the new methodology was the development of a dynamic empowering learning community that could only be termed an "Interactive Cognitive Economy" (an "Interactive Cognitive Economy" takes advantage of the unity of collaboration, with meaningful relevance to subject matter and content, the delivery of challenging and engaging learning activities, though the lens of relevant and meaningful performance objectives and goals). In a "technologically engineered interactive cognitive economy" faculty and students become active learners who are consciously engaged in building, developing, creating, changing, challenging, and advocating. By combining experiences and viewpoints with instructional design, technology, interactivity, discovery, relevance, collaboration, creativity, and innovation new heights were in academics and self—awareness. The new instructional methodology was titled: "Technology Engineering."

The courses that were "Technologically Engineered" were EDU 3700: Statistical Methodology for the Social and Behavioral Sciences (undergraduate) EDGR 5910: Statistical Methodology for the Social and Behavioral Sciences (graduate). The courses were taught in three different methods over a period of two years (2003 to 2005) traditionally, at a distance, and web-enhanced. Courses were provided by both the School of Education (traditional and web-enhanced) and the University College (distance education) of North Carolina Central University. The courses utilized instructional methods and strategies that took full advantage of the Internet Resources, Virtual Chatting, Virtual Assessments, Competence Mastery Tests, Interactive Media, Virtual Classrooms, Electronic Mail, and Discussion Forums to build a strong sense of unity amongst the learners. The goal of the courses (both graduate and undergraduate) was to make the Statistics course content meaningful, relevant, engaging and empowering.

TECHNOLOGY ENGINEERING DEVELOPS AN EFFECTIVE ERGONOMIC LEARNER-CENTERED APPROACH TO TEACHING: "A DYNAMIC INTERACTIVE COGNITIVE ECONOMY"

Teaching can best be described as "The Profession of Empowering." It is often underrated, unheralded, and unappreciated. It is a process of constant extremes. It can be simultaneously frustrating and joyous or dramatic and foreboding. At every level, virtually all teachers agree that the process of teaching can be at times both difficult and rewarding.

Teachers face constant challenges. Yet, with a nurturing and pioneering spirit a teacher can become an interactive agent in a lifelong career of empowering others. It is at this ultimate height that the profession of teaching boasts of workers who are tremendously dedicated and intrinsically motivated. These qualities are so much a part of the profession that despite the many challenges (and many times against the greatest of odds) teachers often succeed and produce astounding results (Osler, 2006).

In terms of curriculum, many of the difficulties that teachers often encounter can be typically found in two major areas. The first area of concern is the transfer of content to the learner and the second area of concern is the student's ability to perform (at a required or specified level) with the new knowledge. Further difficulty can develop when the instructor requires the student to think critically and/or apply content and knowledge to a given situation (thus demonstrating the ability to synthesize and expound upon data).

There are a plethora of teaching strategies and methodologies that may be applied and utilized in any instructional setting. Many of these strategies are concerned with the methodologies of how information is disseminated, delivered, and processed. In many cases, an instructor may devise their own unique strategies to meet the demands of a given learning environment or situation when no other strategies or methodologies are available.

Some teaching methods place an emphasis on rote lecture; others may emphasize learning styles, performance criteria or a systematic approach. It is this author's hope that through a "Technology Engineering" methodology that involves the effective combination of technology (such as Interactive Hypermedia Learning Modules [Interactive Hypermedia and Interactive Graphic User Interfaces], Online Tools [Websites, Webquests, Blogs, and RSS feeds] and Asynchronous Learning Networks [Course Shells, ePortfolio data storage systems, and data management networks]) educators will have access to a plethora of resources that will aid them in developing effective learning environments. Hopefully, through the use of effective Technology Engineering the art of teaching will become efficient, effective, and empowering to both the teacher and the learner (Osler, 2006).

TECHNOLOGY ENGINEERING ELEMENTS

Many institutions are now finding that it is more marketable to reach learners who would not normally have the opportunity to engage in traditional classroom instruction at the University level. There is growing acceptance for the view that educating students beyond the campus is a major element of a University's mission (Harris, 1999). This view is sustained by the enhanced capacity for efficient and widespread use of distance education through advanced electronic delivery systems. Many schools are moving rapidly toward the use of technology to deliver courses and programs at a distance. Distance Education does not simply just refer to computers as the only delivery method of instruction. Several distance education models are presently in use, such as broadcast television, video and audio teleconferencing, and Asynchronous Learning Networks.

Learners use computers and communications technologies in asynchronous learning networks to work with remote learning resources, including online content, as well as instructors, and other learners, but without the requirement to be online at the same time. The most common asynchronous learning network communication tool is the internet through Universal Resource Location (URLs) via Hypertext Topical Protocols (http) for the World Wide Web. The World Wide Web can used in conjunction with e-Learning software such as Blackboard or WebCT. These two asynchronous learning networks can provide University undergraduate and graduate students and their respective instructors with electronic access to course materials, lesson plans, electronic mail, website development tools, grades, activities, and a plethora of communications options such as discussion boards, email, and chat rooms.

THE RATIONAL FOR THE ONLINE
TECHNOLOGY ENGINEERING SOLUTION

Distance Education although a great resource for learning is not without its share of problems. One area of concern is that dropout rates tend to be higher in distance education programs than in traditional face-to-face programs. Carr noted that dropout rates are often 10 to 20 percentage points higher in distance education courses than in traditional courses (Carr, 2000). She also reported significant variation among institutions, with some post-secondary schools reporting course-completion rates of more than 80 percent, while others report fewer than 50 percent of distance education students finish their courses. There are a number of well-documented reasons for some dropouts, including the fact that adults sometimes only register for a course in order to obtain knowledge, not credit, and may therefore drop the course once they obtain the knowledge they desire. These are significant factors that must be taken into account when a University is planning to implement a distance Education course.

An additional concern is the actual physical separation of students in programs offered at a distance. This may also contribute to higher dropout rates in Distance Education courses. The separation of students from their peers, instructor, and a traditional classroom can at times be a factor in the loss of a sense of community. Kerka states that Distance Education has a tendency to reduce the sense of community, giving rise to feelings of disconnection (Kerka, 1996). Also feelings of isolation, distraction, and lack of personal attention can manifest (Besser & Donahue, 1996; Twigg, 1997), which could negatively affect student persistence in distance education courses or programs.

THE TECHNOLOGY ENGINEERING SOLUTIONS FOR THE HURRICANE KATRINA REGION: A FACE TO FACE INTERACTIVE LAB CONDUCTED IN THE REGION BY INSPIREWORKS © AND AN ONLINE INFORMATION NETWORK IN THE SCHOOL OF EDUCATION AT NORTH CAROLINA CENTRAL UNIVERSITY

This Chapter will provide two technology solutions that exemplify outstanding Technology Engineering. These solutions have and can provide aid education in the Hurricane Katrina region. The face to face solution was been implemented and occurred in Shreveport, Louisiana with the Praise Temple Full Gospel Baptist Church by InspireWorks © and was called InspireCamp ©. The online solution is currently being developed as an online resource on the content management system (an Asynchronous Learning Network or "ALN" called Blackboard 7.0) in the School of Education at North Carolina Central University.

THE FACE TO FACE TECHNOLOGY ENGINEERING SOLUTION: INSPIRECAMP © BY INSPIREWORKS ©

The Inspire Works Headquarters

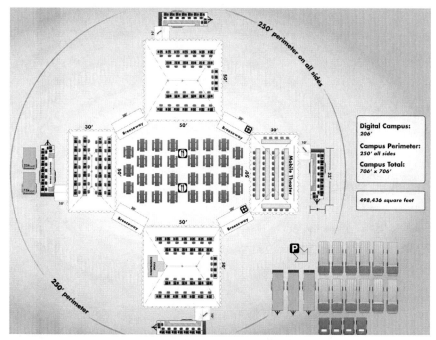

The *InspireCamp* © Structure

InpsireWorks © is a software development and technology company based in Florham Park, New Jersey and Cary, North Carolina. Jim Tagliareni founded InspireWorks ©, in May 2002, and his vision and mission were to move beyond the traditional data tools and processes that were prevalent in industry at that time. Mr. Tagliareni assembled a dynamic development team that had many years of experience in delivering infrastructure platforms and applications for computer systems.

The InspireWorks © team at the time in which the Hurricane Katrina disaster occurred had built a code base for an on-demand horizontal computerized system that served several vertical markets: Education, Sports, Entertainment, Advertising, and the Corporate arena. One area of this horizontal system (which was specifically designed for the education market), is called InspireCamp ©, a digital day camp that had been running across the country.

InspireWorks © enjoyed the summer of 2005 providing digital day camps in the state of New Jersey and partnering with a program sponsored by the New Jersey State Attorney General's Office, called "Project Vision—Adventure Club." "Project Vision—Adventure Club" were technology-based camps for children. These camps allowed children to create digital film projects reflecting life experiences.

The InspireCamp © Interior

When the Hurricane Katrina Disaster took place InspireWorks © decided to offer help to the gulf coast residents affected by Hurricane Katrina. Jim Tagliareni decided that InspireWorks © would go to the gulf coast region and set up a fun after-school digital day camp for school children ranging in ages 5 to 18 (or K—12th grade). The technology camp was set up in Shreveport, Louisiana as an collaborative effort with the Praise Temple Full Gospel Baptist Church. Praise Temple made available over 2 acres of land to establish the digital campus. The camp was operated by InspireWorks' employees and volunteers. The camp facilities were made up of 150 computer workstations, four 50-foot tents with breezeways, 3 mobile video production studios, and an eating area designed to seat up to 300 individuals.

The camp curriculum was set up with 10 interactive modules. Topics ranged from Introduction to the Digital Production Process, Script Writing, DVD Authoring, I AM, to specialty courses, such as Earth Science. The children partnered in groups to create personal DVDs, each with constructivist hands-on time on the computer. The goal of the Shreveport camp was to provide a diversion from the recent events brought on by Hurricane Katrina and to give the children a different outlet; knowledge of the digital process, and a way to deal with life's challenges by re-emphasizing the importance of education. In addition, the camp included remedial tutorials in mathematics and

The InspireCamp © in Action

language arts. A special time set aside for the students to complete their assignments and homework, specialized sessions took place on life skills and ethical sessions were conducted that placed emphasis on good morals.

Several keynote speakers were invited and motivated and encouraged the campers as well as the community. Invited speakers included: Senate Chaplain Barry Black, Dr. Wintley Phipps, Bishop Paul S. Morton, and Bishop W. Todd Ervin. Each offered rousing, power-packed, and encouraging messages. On Friday of each week, the camp finale was conducted and concluded with the presentation of the personal DVDs created by the children which were shown to their parents, friends, community and citywide leaders. The InspireCamp © was a success and greatly aided in the residents in the region in enhancing their quality of life.

THE ONLINE TECHNOLOGY ENGINEERING SOLUTION: THE HURRICANE KATRINA ONLINE EDUCATIONAL NETWORK © A RESOURCE FOR TEACHERS

Educators who perceive the value of social bonds in the learning environment can envision and conceptualize how a sense of community can be stimulated

Chapter Seven

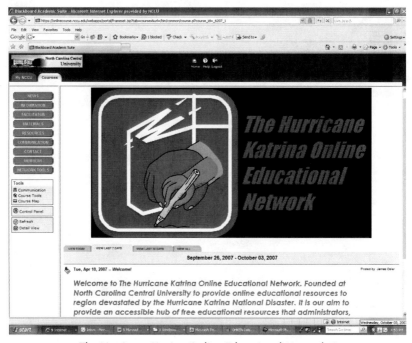

The Hurricane Katrina Online Educational Network ©

in virtual classrooms, particularly in Internet-based asynchronous learning network courses and content management systems. The purpose of The Hurricane Katrina Online Educational Network © is to provide an online digital Resource for Teachers in the hurricane Katrina region.

Through this newly created centralized educational online resource teachers in the Hurricane affected region will soon be able to interact with peers and colleagues throughout the country through the use of asynchronous learning network tools such as text-based discussion boards, document posting options, website tools, electronic mail, and virtual classrooms (that feature graphical presentation tools and virtual chat rooms). These tools allow teachers to interact and communicate with each other without being present and without the requirement of always being online at the same time. Combining asynchronous learning networks with creative course development resources can create a dynamic and energetic learning network that promotes discovery, creativity, and sharing. The aforementioned factors are known to enhance the formation of a community, and thereby demonstrate that a sense of community can be created in an asynchronous learning network environment.

There is an old African saying that states, "It takes a village to raise a child." The same statement may be made in regards to the provision of teaching resources and aid via asynchronous learning network/course management systems. A dynamic teaching methodology that works in concert along with the functions of an asynchronous learning network can develop a strong community of teachers and provide them with rapidly with much needed resources. This in turn, allows educators to greatly broaden the scope and reach of education.

Interest in community and community learning is not limited to the field of education. The last few decades have witnessed an increase in interest in the concept of "community" in general. Much of this interest is based on the perception that sense of community in the United States is weak and there is a need to get American citizens to think about working together toward the common good (Etzioni, 1993). John Goodlad of the University of Washington, head of the Institute for Educational Renewal (1997), echoed these sentiments when he quoted an editorial from the 1990 issue of the Holistic Education. Goodlad (1997) stated:

> *"Our culture does not nourish that which is best or noblest in the human spirit. It does not cultivate vision, imagination, or aesthetic or spiritual sensitivity. It does not encourage gentleness, generosity, caring, or compassion. Increasingly in the late twentieth century, the economic-technocratic-static worldview has become a monstrous destroyer of what is loving and life-affirming in the human soul." (p. 125)*

This point of view is echoed by many modern educators who feel the same about evolving traditional modes of teaching and instruction. Research provides evidence that strong feelings of community may not only increase persistence in courses, but may also increase the flow of information among all learners, availability of support, commitment to group goals, cooperation among members, and satisfaction with group efforts (Bruffee, 1993; Dede, 1996; Wellman, 1999). Additionally, learners benefit from community membership by experiencing a greater sense of well being and by having an agreeable set of individuals to call on for support when needed (Walker, Wasserman & Wellman, 1994; Wellman & Gulia, 1999). Researchers Royal and Rossi suggest that learners' sense of community is related to their engagement in school activities, with students who have a higher sense of community being less likely to experience class cutting behavior or thoughts of dropping out of school and more likely to report feeling bad when unprepared for classes. Additionally, they report that students reporting a high sense of community less often feel burned out at school (Royal and Rossi, 1996).

Tinto supported the findings of Royal and Rossi when he emphasized the importance of community in reducing dropouts when he theorized that students will increase their levels of satisfaction and the likelihood of persisting in a college program if they feel involved and develop relationships with other members of the learning community (Tinto, 1993). This important research can be used to support the building of learning communities via asynchronous learning networks. Thus, empirical research supports the importance of community. Wehlage, Rutter and Smith (1989) found that traditional schools with exemplary dropout-prevention programs devoted considerable attention to overcoming the barriers that prevented students from connecting with the school and to developing a sense of belonging, membership, and engagement. The key finding of their report is that effective schools provide students with a "supportive community." In a study of adult learners in a work-site GED program, researchers Vann and Hinton (1994) found that 84 percent of completers belonged to class cliques, whereas 70 percent of dropouts were socially isolated. A final example, Ashar and Skenes (1993) found in a higher education business program that by creating a social environment that motivated adult learners to persist, social integration had a significant positive effect on retention. The research uncovered that learning needs alone appeared strong enough to attract adults to the program, but not to retain them (Ashar and Skenes, 1993).

Courses and resources that are offered via online networking programs (Asynchronous Learning Networks/Course management Systems) can be used in conjunction with interactive and dynamic teaching strategies to create a strong sense of community. This model may be very advantageous to the Hurricane Katrina and Rita regions were non-traditional means of resources may be the answer to a lack of infrastructure that greatly affects the learning environment. Currently, the Massachusetts Institute of Technology (MIT) has a $100.00 Laptop initiative that uses the internet to provide content. This initiative in conjunction with the use of the Technology Engineered solutions such as InspireWorks © InspireCamp ©, The Hurricane Katrina Online Educational Network © could rebuild the learning environment in the hurricane region in a proactive, positive, and progressive way.

CONCLUSION

Technology Engineering is an empowering philosophy, practice, and methodology that combines resources and computing with an interactive and dynamic instructional strategies. It can be used empower both students and teachers in the Hurricane Katrina region who can readily take advantage of the resources to improve their lives and rebuild their learning environment. As we continue to grow and develop in education, the proper use and implementation of innovative and interactive technology is providing educators with new territory to explore and new resources to share.

Sharing of time and resources can prove to be invaluable to those affected by natural disasters. In many cases it can literally make a difference with those who are suffering from extreme loss. As we explore and share in this new arena of Technology Engineering we make the art of teaching more effective, more valuable, more dynamic, and more accessible. The results can be rather dramatic. Students who may have once been intimidated by the course content and teachers who may have once lacked vital resources; can transform into pioneering giants. They may now bristle with confidence, when they were once broken by traumatic experiences. Effective Technology Engineering at its very core is an art that is composed of just the right combination of: curriculum, creativity, technology, and the profound desire to share through love.

In the "Information Age" we are boundless and as limitless as our imagination. New pedagogical and andragogical methods are being developed by those who interact and teach students with technological tools. Technology Engineering has the ability to transform individuals, environments, and institutions. The end results may prove to be as far reaching as the early printing press and have the unlimited potential to take the art of teaching to previously unforeseen heights. Thus, our future is bright and the positive implications are limitless.

REFERENCES

Ashar, H. and Skenes, R., 1993. Can Tinto's Student Departure Model be Applied to Nontraditional Students? *Adult Education Quarterly*, Vol. 43, No. 2, pp. 90–100.

Besser, H. and Donahue, S., 1996. Introduction and Overview: Perspectives on Distance Independent Education, *Journal of the American Society for Information Science*, Vol. 47, No. 11, pp. 801–804.

Bruffee, K. A., 1993. *Collaborative Learning: Higher Education, Interdependence, and the Authority of Knowledge.* John Hopkins University Press, Baltimore, USA.

Carr, S., 2000. As Distance Education Comes of Age, the Challenge is Keeping the Students. *The Chronicle of Higher Education*, Vol. 46, No. 23, pp. A39-A41.

Dede, C., 1996. The Evolution of Distance Education: Emerging Technologies and Distributed Learning. *American Journal of Distance Education*, Vol. 10, No. 2, pp. 4–36.

Downing, D. (1987). Dictionary of Mathematical Terms. Hauppauge, NY: Barron's Educational Series, Inc.

Etzioni, A., 1993. *The Spirit of Community: Rights, Responsibility, and the Communitarian Agenda.* Crown, New York, USA.

Galaskiewicz J. and Wasserman S., 1994. Advances in Social Network Analysis. *SAGE Focus Editions*. Vol. 171, pp. 53–78.

Goodlad, J. L., 1997. *In Praise of Education.* Teachers College Press, New York, USA.

Harris, D. A., 1999. Online Distance Education in the United States, *IEEE Communications Magazine*, Vol. 37, No. 3, pp. 87–91.

Jacobson, L., 2006. Hurricanes' aftermath is ongoing. *Education Week.* Vol. 25, No. 21, 1–18.

Kerka, S., 1996. *Distance learning, the Internet, and the World Wide Web.* Education Resources Information Center, Lanham, USA.

Osler, J. E. (2005). *Technology Engineering: Developing, implementing, and infusing interactive hypermedia learning modules into an asynchronous learning network to develop an interactive community of learners.* Interactive Presentation and Paper Presented at The 2005 South Atlantic Philosophy of Education Society Refereed Annual Yearbook.

Osler, J. E. (2006). *Technology Engineering: a paradigm shift to promote academic freedom in the information age.* The South Atlantic Philosophy of Education Society Refereed Annual Yearbook.

Royal, M.A. and Rossi, R.J., 1996. Individual-Level Correlates of Sense of Community: Findings from Workplace and School. *Journal of Community Psychology,* Vol. 24, No. 4, pp. 395–416.

Tinto, V., 1993. *Leaving college: Rethinking the causes and cures of student attrition.* University of Chicago Press., Chicago, USA.

Twigg, C.A., 1997. Is Technology a Silver Bullet? *Educom Review,* Vol. 31, No. 2, pp. 28–29.

Vann, B. A. et al, 1994. Workplace Social Networks and Their Relationship to Student Retention in On-Site GED Programs. *Human Resource Development Quarterly,* Vol. 5, No. 2, pp. 141–51.

United States Department of Education (2006). *Supporting Americans affected by hurricane Katrina.* www.ed.gov/katrina.

Walker, J. et al, 1994. Statistical Models for Social Support Networks. *SAGE Focus Editions.* Vol. 171, pp. 40–53.

Wellman, B., 1999. *Networks in the Global Village.* Westview Press, Boulder, USA.

Wellman, B., 1999. *Networks in the Global Village: The Network Community: An Introduction to Networks in the Global Village.* Westview Press, Boulder, USA.

Wellman, B. and Gulia, M., 1999. *Networks in the Global Village: The Network Basis of Social Support: A Network is More than the Sum of its Ties.* Westview Press, Boulder, USA.

Chapter Eight

Hurricane Katrina Survivors: Telling My Story

Dorothy M. Singleton and Deborah B. Eaton

TELLING MY STORY #1
MAY 7, 2006

As we walked through certain parts of New Orleans, Louisiana, especially the Ninth Ward, we were devastated by seeing so much debris left behind from Hurricane Katrina, just a year ago. In the midst of all which had taken place, the people of New Orleans were willing to tell their story. During the Sunday morning service at a local church, many people talked of hope and spiritual strength. The minister made several references, in his sermon, to the book of John 1:1–4. The scripture reads as:

In the beginning was the Word, and the Word was with God, and the Word was God. The same was in the beginning with God. All things were made by him; and without him was not any thing made that was made. In him was life; and the life was the light of man. Other scriptures were cited, in the minister's sermon, such as John 6:63; John 10:10; John 14:6; 1John 5:12; and Matthew 6:33.
In sharing this scripture is to attest to the sovereignty of God. Certainly the people of the Gulf Coast region must find comfort in remembering and understanding the power of God in their situation in light of their experiences of Katrina.

We met several people at church. We arrived at church approximately 11:45am. The people were very nice and appeared faithful to their beliefs. We were given a welcome packet as visitors to the church. During this time, we were told that we will receive a free tape on the morning sermon if we filled out the information sheet in the packet. The church was lively and spirit filled. The minister was very jolly and extremely animated. We were focusing on the topic of the sermon *"Prepare for Life."* The minister spoke about different cultures within the churches; talked about the Holy dance. To him, culture is described as how we worship God; spiritual extension of our own culture; culturally responsive to the environment of the church. He stated that spirituality is something not seen; God has prepared us for life. God wants you to experience what has been done.

After the sermon, six young ladies joined the church. After church, we exited the sanctuary. A lady, about fifty years of age, embraced me. I'll call her Ms Sue. She said, "I love your spirit." We talked for a short period of time. Afterwards, we moved to the basement of the church where we met the minister's wife. We talked about the Christian School which they are organizing within their church. The minister and his wife expressed their concerns about the public schools and what they did not provide for children in the area before Hurricane Katrina. The minister's wife is now home-schooling their children. The minister stated that they don't like what's going on in the schools and they do not want their children to be a part of it.

Many survivors talked about God and being hopeful that God will get them through this situation.

TELLING MY STORY #2
MRS. C'S WORLD: LIVING IN A BOX BUT HOPEFUL

Mrs. C, a woman about 45 years old, is a survivor of Hurricane Katrina. We met Mrs. C on May 7, 2006 as we were driving through neighborhoods right after church. She was outside of her home doing yard work-moving debris. We offered to help her. She was surprised—strangers offering to assist her. She was wonderful and engaging as we talked about her situation (living in a FEMA trailer) which was placed in front of her home. She lived in the trailer with her husband and fourteen year old daughter. Mrs. C's husband is working and her daughter is enrolled in one of the schools in New Orleans. Mrs. C is not pleased with the high school which her daughter has been assigned. The daughter is very unhappy with her assignment. She doesn't want to go to school because all of her friends have moved away. Mrs. C said her daughter is being rebellious. At 14, this is a time which children show this behavior. However, Mrs. C is a very positive individual who is employed and is trying to restore her home. She hopes to move into her home soon.

Mrs. C invited us into her home. She took us through her home which was or had been filled with water from Hurricane Katrina. The water rose just beneath the window frame; the water was above her dining room table. The house was smelly. She was using a special kind of disinfectant (solution) to get rid of the mold.

Mrs. C is a Christian woman who strongly believes in God. She is going to make it and be blessed with more than she had before Hurricane Katrina. Mrs. C's faith is incredible. She talked about her experiences in Dallas, TX which she stayed with a niece of the family; they were given the royal treatment for one (1) week and were then told to leave. Afterwards, they moved to Donaldson to her daughter's (an older daughter) sister-in-law house and were then told to move two days later.

Mrs. C told of her experiences at the Superdome—*Promises Made, Promises Broken*. People had to pretend something was wrong with them in order for those in charge to do things for them. People pretend they were ill; they were acting delirious; anything to get attention. Mrs. C stated that after Hurricane Katrina, she has been able to read three books and recommended that we read them as well. The books are as follows:

- He Came to Set the Captives Free,
- The Devine Revelation of Hell by Marion Baxter, and
- Deluge by Douglas Brinkley

To me, these books were means of survival, said Mrs. C. She said that people were told that there were many (50 or more buses) buses to take them to the Convention Center. It was a LIE!!! There were three buses waiting to transfer people. People at the Superdome had food. Those being transferred to the Convention Center did not. There were several crimes committed at the Superdome, such as sex, rapes, shooting and other crimes contrary to what people say.

Mrs. C was standing in her mobile home, given by the Federal Emergency Management Agency (FEMA), when she was telling us about her experiences. Four of us were in a space which was probably designated comfortably for two people. The mobile home was extremely small. There's no comparison to what they lived in as a family of three in a very modest home. Mrs. C has hope, faith and love in the mighty God we serve.

TELLING MY STORY #3
DIALOGUE WITH MR. DJ

As we traveled through the Ninth Ward of New Orleans, we managed to get lost. We stopped for directions at a local one-stop store. We asked for directions. Two gentlemen provided those directions to us. After getting those directions, we started asking questions about the Hurricane Katrina ordeal and also questions about the current Mayor of New Orleans. Mr. DJ was very candid about his responses. He is the owner of a remodeling & repair Service Company. Mr. DJ was very curious about us. He asked several questions such as: 1) Where are you from? What are your perceptions of things after the hurricane? Why are black people not crossing over economically? Of course, Mr. DJ had several responses to the questions he was asking. He stated that:

> *"As a people we don't trust each other and Hurricane Katrina has revealed the ills of society. The hurricane was a great revelation of revealing sickness; the problems were already here before the storm."*

Again, we began to ask him several more questions such as 1) what are your perceptions about the mayor? Mr. DJ's response was:

> *"He is a figure-head. The mayor and the governor are in this together; there is no procedure in place to help us. Many Blacks want a free ride; free houses, clothes; blacks have become dependent on the system. He further stated that Black people have a docile behavior. They are fearful of the unknown; they are fearful of failure/success; and their answer to the situation is to do nothing."*

> *"People have to define their space. They need to establish boundaries. Efforts have been individual and not collective. Mr. DJ had several topics of discussion. They were based on local politics, crime in New Orleans, and celebrities seeking information."*

TELLING MY STORY #4
DIALOGUE WITH MS. K

Ms. K's mother is famous for the Hurricane Katrina's article which was printed in the Washington Post a month after the hurricane flooded New Orleans. Ms. K talked about realtors coming to New Orleans asking to purchase as much land as possible. The offer for each lot was $40,000.00. Individuals were given $40,000.00 for their land and/or house. Ms. K equated that to 40 acres and a mule.

Ms. K complained about the city rebuilding Rally's restaurant and MacDonald's in two days; but couldn't assist in building homes nor assist in getting help for the people of New Orleans. Since the disaster in New Orleans, Ms. K has moved to several places to seek employment. She moved to Vancouver, Washington and was treated well by the people there. She stated that:

> *"The people in New Orleans did not care about others who have lived there all of their lives."*

When she lived in Vancouver, Ms. K was assisted in getting a rent-free, three bedroom apartment. Ms. K has since returned to New Orleans and is currently working at Emeril's restaurant.

MY STORY #5
THOMAS

Thomas was on a rooftop of an apartment complex for 4 days with 2000 other people, without food and water. He was there to rescue as many people as possible. At this time, Thomas' girlfriend experienced a miscarriage. Prior to the hurricane, Thomas' family had moved to Baton Rouge. Thomas stated that he will not sell his property in New Orleans and that he plans to rebuild his house as well as his life.

"God is good and He will open many doors to those who believe. . . "